Do We Have A Center?

2016, 2020, and the Challenge
of the Trump Presidency

Walter Frank

LRD Press

ISBN: 978-0-578-54105-1
Library of Congress Control Number: 2019909803

LRD Press
41 Riverside Drive
Princeton, New Jersey 08540
wltr.frank@gmail.com

Praise for Other Works by the Author

Law and the Gay Rights Story

"The balance of deep treatment of legal issues, vivid event coverage, honest critiques of the movement, and particular attention to the individuals who faced enormous risks fighting for gay rights makes this book an engaging and meaningful read."

—HARVARD LAW REVIEW

Making Sense of the Constitution

"an engaging and readable study of how and why the Court does what it does and with what intellectual and other resources, when it interprets the constitutional text. Frank has read widely and he cogently but lightly responds to claims and counterclaims by presenting the findings of many scholars."

—JETHRO LIEBERMAN IN THE
POLITICAL SCIENCE QUARTERLY

For Eva, Jacob, Nathan, and Zachary

Acknowledgments

First, let me simply express my deep appreciation to a number of scholars for their comments, criticisms, suggestions and support. Whatever shortcomings diminish this work would have been greater but for their generosity. I would like to thank in particular Hal Feiveson, Robert Freidin, Stan Katz, Ed Rubin, Stephen Skowronek, Jeff Tulis, Dan Wood, and Mike Zuckerman. Thanks also to the wonderful journalist Tish Durkin for her insightful thoughts on the manuscript.

Second, I am blessed with numerous friends whose judgment I value and who allowed me to inflict earlier drafts of the manuscript on them. Their comments were also very helpful. In this connection, let me express my special gratitude to Gary Mailman, Steve Newman, and David Vilkomerson.

Finally, I extend a special thanks to my wife, Lydia, for not complaining as I monopolized the computer and for simply being the person she is. As much as we both love books, we know that there are a few things even more important.

Table of Contents

INTRODUCTION xi

PART I: 2016 1

    Chapter 1 The Story 3

    Chapter 2 2016: The Autopsy 66

PART II: TODAY AND TOMORROW 141

    Chapter 3 Where we are now 143

    Chapter 4 Looking to November 3, 2020 171

REFERENCES 199

APPENDICES 206

    Appendix I: Excerpts from Announcement Speeches
    of Hillary Clinton and Donald J. Trump. 206

    Appendix II: Excerpts from Announcement Speeches
    of Three Leading Democratic Candidates in 2020 213

    Appendix III: State Election Polls in Swing States
    in the 10 days before the 2016 Presidential Election...... 223

    Appendix IV – Additional Perspectives on Polarization 227

    Appendix V: Memories – 1952 and 1960. 231

Introduction

Politics was once described as the art of the possible. It no longer feels that way. Today, it seems more like a battle between two feudal armies. Part of this book aims at showing it doesn't have to be that way. Polarization didn't start with Trump and it won't end with him unless we can somehow rescue the country from the political ditch into which it has fallen. So another purpose of this book is to examine just how we got here and how the Democrats, with the right kind of message and an appealing candidate, can lead the way to a more sensible politics.

In 2016, however, Hillary Clinton made a terrible mistake: she thought she could win if she simply replicated the Obama coalition. She was wrong, and examining why she was wrong, how she misunderstood the electorate, and how and why an outsider like Donald Trump turned out to be the more effective candidate is also a key purpose of this effort.

In 2012 author and columnist Gail Collins wrote: "... there is virtually nothing, no matter how crazy, that you can't get 18 percent of Americans to support if they're in a bad enough mood." Her proof? "In the spring of 2011, 17 percent of likely Republican primary voters said they thought it would be a good idea to nominate Donald Trump for president" (GC 13). Five years later, of course, almost half the country must have been in a very sour mood, electing Donald Trump the forty-fifth President of the United States.

So how did a notion deemed so preposterous in 2011 that Collins thought it a marker for lunacy become our political reality in 2016? And what kind of nation have we become? Are we really divided into two armed camps as many commentators and politicians would have us believe? Is there, as the title of this book asks, still a center worth worrying about in today's politics?

These are important questions not only for understanding the recent past but because they bear importantly on what may happen in 2020 and, even more importantly, on the future direction of the country.

Let me give you a slightly more detailed roadmap for our journey together.

Chapter 1 recounts the events of the 2016 general election. It is an important exercise even if painful for those like myself who did not support the winning candidate. Although the racist overtones of Trump's campaign were deeply disturbing, it would be a mistake to overlook the many ways in which his team ran a better campaign than Hillary Clinton's, better focused strategically and organizationally, much more attuned to what was actually going on in the country, playing better to the candidate's strengths, and with much better lines of communication and decision-making.

Over the last two years, I have examined most all the literature relating to the 2016 election, everything from memoirs and journalistic retellings to statistically laden academic studies. The results of that effort are reflected in Chapter 2. I begin with a question: are we as polarized as we seem to think and, if so, how did we get that way. Next, I examine the nature of Trump's appeal, why he struck such a strong emotional chord with so many. Several studies seek an explanation for Trump's success in white racial anxiety. I don't find them persuasive and explain why. Finally, I address all the different aspects of the race that might have made a difference in the outcome. Trump's victory had many contributors from then-FBI Director James Comey to Green Party candidate Jill Stein, from the Russians to the dynamics of social media. We examine all these factors and others as well.

The novelist William Kennedy has written "the man of power achieves power only because he fulfills the needs of others in both obvious and secret ways" (WK 168). Just how Trump fulfilled those needs is the overarching story of Chapters 1 and 2 and provides an important backdrop to the 2020 election.

Chapter 3 begins by placing Trump in the larger context of our history using the framework of noted political scientist Stephen Skowronek. I see Trump's relentless undermining of our most important institutions and norms as potentially very dangerous, particularly if he is re-elected. I also, however, emphasize the strength of our federalist structure and even briefly look back at the progressive era to remind readers that the nation has faced many of the same problems we face today — including rising income inequality, the consolidation of corporate power, and the challenges of immigration. The balance of Chapter 3 makes the case for a more centrist politics, defining centrism not as a place on the political spectrum but as a mindset for how we approach politics itself. The cards are currently stacked against the kind of politics I seek and I show how online media has been particularly complicit in this development. I also suggest how it can play a more constructive role in 2020.

Chapter 4 focuses on the 2020 presidential campaign. I briefly discuss Governor William Weld's challenge to Trump and how Trump, if he were a different person, might actually use their contest as a way of enhancing his appeal to the broader electorate. Trump will be an extremely formidable candidate and I describe some of the advantages he will enjoy. The main business of the Chapter, however, deals with the Democrats, describing what I believe they must do and not do to defeat Trump in 2020.

I've written this book because I think we are at a pivotal moment in our history, one that requires us to understand both our recent past and the fundamental nature of the choice we will be facing in 2020. One can find Trump's campaign message deeply disturbing and in many cases deceitful, but the fact remains that Donald Trump was in many ways the superior candidate in 2016. I don't think anyone can read the first two chapters and not come to a similar conclusion though I didn't set out to prove a particular point one way or the other. I also believe, however, that Trump has proven to be a deeply flawed President — flawed in such ways that, if legitimized by his re-election, will make the dysfunctional course of our politics even more difficult to reverse. It is why I offer my own thoughts suggesting a path for victory for the Democrats in 2020.

I have been around a long time. If you had told the fifteen year old Walter in 1960 that there would be no war in Europe for the balance of my lifetime, that the Soviet Union would simply disappear without the firing of a single shot, that the systematic legal oppression of African Americans in our American South would finally meet its end, that by the end of the decade we would have a man on the moon and that decades later we could carry in our pocket a device that would let me immediately access the accumulated knowledge of all mankind while reminding my sister living in Perth Australia of the dates of our impending visit, all while sitting on the 104 bus making its way down Broadway, I would probably have looked around for a policeman or simply hurried on my way.

We have every reason to be smart. We have no reason to despair.

Part I: 2016

Chapter 1

The Story

In mid-November 2018, President Trump referred to Congressman Adam Schiff, the soon to be chair of the House Intelligence Committee, as Adam *Schitt*. At virtually the same time, he attacked the Navy Seal Commander who led the raid that killed Osama bin Laden, the architect of the attacks of September 11, 2001, accusing him of being a Clinton supporter and asserting that bin Laden should have been killed sooner. It was just a typical day in the Trump White House.

Two years into his presidency at the time, neither comment surprised anyone. In his nomination fight, Trump turned Ronald Reagan's rule — I shall speak ill of no fellow Republican — on its head, speaking well of no one and asking, for example, whether anyone with a television in their house could ever vote for Carly Fiorina ("Look at that face. Would anyone vote for that?"). No target was too respected (He belittled Senator John McCain's years of captivity in Hanoi.) nor any claim too outrageous (He suggested that Senator Ted Cruz of Texas' father was involved in the assassination of President John F. Kennedy).

And yet he is the President.

A couple of weeks after Trump's 2016 victory, Peggy Noonan in her weekly column for the Wall Street Journal, offered a moment of hope for those who wanted to wish well of any incoming President. In it, she related how in the middle of the campaign she needed to check a quote with a member of Trump's staff. The staff member returned her call from Trump Force One. "We spoke," Noonan relates, "and then suddenly the phone seemed to drop and I heard, 'Who's that?' Then I heard, 'Peggy, this is Donald.' Noonan went on:

> I won't quote exactly what was said. No one put it off the record, but it felt off the record, and some of the conversation was personal. But I can describe it. He was dignified, hilarious and modest. He told me that I'd sometimes been unfair to him, sometimes mean, sometimes really, really mean but that when I was he usually deserved it, always appreciated it, and keep it up. He spoke of other things; he characterized for me my career.
>
> I'd heard of his charm offensive, but I'd be lying if I didn't say how charming, funny and frank he was – and, as I say, how modest. How actually humble.
>
> It moved me. And it hurt a few weeks later when I wrote in this space that 'Sane Donald Trump' would win in a landslide but that the one we had long seen, the crazed, shallow one, wouldn't and didn't deserve to.
>
> Is it possible there are deeper reserves of humility, modesty and good intent lurking around in there than we know? And maybe a tool box, too, that can screw those things together and produce something good. (PN)

A charming, funny, humble Trump? Even the most ardent Trump supporter would admit it hasn't turned out that way.

On July 10, 2015, just a few weeks after he entered the race, Trump met with the families of Americans who had been killed by "illegal aliens." It was a staged event. Joel Pollack, a senior editor at Breitbart News, sees it as the moment Trump took control of the 2016 race. Trump first met privately with the families of the victims. Then some family members told their stories at a press conference. Trump refused to back down from his previous comments about race. "By July 19," records Pollack, "just nine days later, Trump had surged to first place [in the nomination battle] and never looked back." In his book, Pollack, a Trump supporter, acknowledges that the number of victims "is very small" but for him the victims and their families "stood for all of the Americans who had been ignored by government for so many years (JP xix-xx)." The border visit symbolized everything that many in his base would cherish about him.

Both Trump and Clinton announced their candidacies in June 2015, a year and a half before the general election. Most Clinton people at this time were hoping Trump would get the nomination. They thought him the weakest candidate and many even doubted that Trump really wanted to win. The conventional wisdom was that he thought a respectable run would enhance his name and be a windfall for his many businesses. They might have thought otherwise if they realized that in November 2012, immediately following Romney's loss, Trump trademarked the slogan "Make America Great Again," or that in January 2015 Trump asked Newt Gingrich to meet him in Iowa for lunch and grilled him for nearly an hour on Gingrich's own experience running for President. Gingrich and others who realized the extent of Trump's presidential ambitions concluded that he was very serious about running.

In his announcement speech, Trump charged that Mexico was exporting its rapists over our borders and promised to build a wall that Mexico would pay for, claimed a net worth of well-over $10 billion, and asserted that "our nuclear arsenal doesn't work." He also predicted "I will be the greatest jobs President God ever created" and "our country needs a truly great leader now. We need a leader that wrote *The Art of the Deal*." And if anyone still doubted his self-confidence there was this: "the American dream is dead – but if I win, I will bring it back bigger and better and stronger than ever."

Hillary Clinton's announcement speech was quintessentially Hillary: cautious, logical, well-organized, and not very exciting. It already sounded her major theme of inclusiveness ("I'm not running for some Americans but for all Americans.") She was at her best when she simply talked about herself and her growing up, how she would help her father in his small business, and how the kindness of others saved her abused and neglected mother. It was clearly an attempt to humanize her. As expected, Clinton made sure that everyone knew her big tent included the women the Republicans "blame and shame" and gays whom the G.O.P. has "turned its back on."

There was a reason that the speech was so bland. It was essentially written by a committee with drafts hurtling back and forth as the deadline approached. Everyone wanted to set just the right tone, say just the right thing — but everyone had slightly different ideas as to how to do it. One speechwriter became so frustrated with the process that he quit a week before the announcement speech but not before delivering a "frank assessment of the shortcomings of the operation and the speech." (JA 16).

In contrast, the Trump people, including Trump himself, were much more focused on how he would look than what he would say. After all, nobody could tell what he was going to say anyway. According to his then campaign manager Corey Lewandowski, Trump's announcement speech might have seemed rambling and disjointed — and it was — but the timing and visuals had been carefully thought out:

> We planned that announcement six weeks ahead of time. We knew what the announcement was going to look like. It's going to look like he was the President of the United States, just flags behind him and a blue carpet, with him in a blue suit and white shirt and a red tie. Everything was very specific. Donald Trump was very specific about the music he would walk into. All of those factors, particularly the look, are very important to Donald Trump (Institute 43).

In June 2015, most everyone expected that Hillary would be the Democratic nominee while the press treated Trump's early announcement almost as an embarrassment. He was given little chance for success. Yet why not Trump? He was the quintessential outsider at a time when gridlock in Washington cast a pall over most politicians and polls showed that voters increasingly regarded long experience in Washington as a negative thing. Trump understood that being outrageous in a celebrity culture is not necessarily a losing formula. Then there was the way he addressed his rallies. He invited his supporters into his world, a world of winners and losers where it was time for America to win again. His tone was part conversational/

part rap. The connection between Trump and his supporters was palpable.

Trump was not far off when he said at a January 2016 rally that he "could stand in the middle of Fifth Avenue and shoot somebody and I wouldn't lose voters." In the end, it seemed that Trump and the other sixteen Republican aspirants were simply not playing the same game. Bush, Kasich, Christie, Cruz, and all the rest addressed their rallies. These rallies were traditional campaign events. Trump's rallies were different. He didn't need to convince his supporters of anything. He was one of them, someone from the other side, the business side, a rich man who talked like no rich man they had ever heard, who shared their anger, their deepest fears, their insecurities and prejudices — and was willing to voice them.

His opponents were tone deaf when it came to what was happening in the Republican Party. Jeb Bush, in an attempt to discredit Trump, called him "the chaos candidate" not realizing that Trump's strongest supporters treated it as a deep compliment. In retrospect, it is fascinating how so few seemed to have taken Trump seriously even among the most conservative Republican voters. Theda Skocpol and Vanessa Williamson, interviewed grass roots Tea Party voters before the Republican primary season began and reported:

> Grassroots tea party involvement in the GOP presidential primaries may also be intense, but may not add up to a united effort for a winning candidate....When Donald Trump was blustering about Obama's birth certificate, he got a chuckle and an "Atta Boy" from some Tea Partiers but no one seemed to take him seriously as a candidate. (TS 194).

Tea Party activists may not have been ideologically in tune with Trump given that free trade and hostility to most social programs were key tenets for them. Nevertheless, Trump's populist rhetoric would certainly have resonated with the anger and outsider status Tea Partiers relished about themselves. The vigor with which Trump attacked both Obamacare and Obama made it easy for even those Tea Partiers initially skeptical about Trump to eventually come over to his side.

A key unrecognized strength for Trump was the breadth of his appeal within the Republican Party. Exit polls showed him winning 39% of those Republicans classifying themselves as very conservative, 46% of the somewhat conservative and 42% of those describing themselves as moderate. (WS 33).

There was something else. Nobody has ever accused Trump of being other than himself. And he insisted on staying that way from the very start of his campaign. He made it a point, for example, to tell his staffers that there should be no effort to hide or downplay his wealth, as Romney had done. "It was," said Lewandowski, "a strategic decision that we made early on." "I'm going to pull up in my 757," Lewandowski recalls Trump saying, "I'm going to make sure everyone sees the giant Trump plane… and we're going to have the most expensive cars, and we're going to do it so everyone understands what this country is all about" (Institute 28), an interesting window into Trump's view of what makes America great..

But now, Trump faced one opponent, not sixteen — and she would no doubt be a formidable adversary.

Until August 2016, Hillary Clinton and Donald Trump had inhabited two different worlds for their entire lives. Hers had been the world of law, government, politics, and public service, while his was one of real estate deals and public celebrity. Each had been deeply shaped by their experiences. For Trump, real estate is a zero-sum game. There are winners and losers. It is fiercely competitive and you have to take risks just to survive and to be a player. In real estate, there is only so much land and only so many development projects to go around. Trump was once asked what money meant to him after his first billion. He said it was important, but only as a way of keeping score.

As for Hillary, we should never forget that in 1988 and again in 1991 the *National Law Journal* ranked her as one of the country's most influential lawyers and for years she was one of only a handful of women litigating cases in Arkansas. Her legal instincts promised to be both a blessing and a curse. On the positive side, she was (and still is) incredibly smart and a world-class listener. On the negative side, at least as a candidate, the one thing all lawyers learn early on is that you never ask a question in cross-examining a witness unless you already know the answer. Lawyers stick to the script but candidates have to improvise. Even take risks. But that did not seem to be in her nature.

The ultimate world-view of the two candidates could not have been more different. Trump once said, "Man is the most vicious of all animals and life is a series of battles ending in victory or defeat. You just can't let people make a sucker out of you." (DA). Hillary had written *It Takes a Village*.

Though both candidates had wrapped up their nominations by June, nobody knew what to expect of the conventions. This was, after all, going to be a general election fight between two presidential candidates with the highest negative ratings in the history of modern American politics.

How had such candidates snatched the great prize for their own? There is no denying that each had enjoyed a bit of luck. The fact that at the outset no one took Trump seriously was undoubtedly an advantage. Most of the time when candidates aren't regarded as viable, they are ignored. In Trump's case, however, given his celebrity status, the media, in the colorful words of journalist Tish Durkin, "spent the first three quarters of the primary process being treated as a fireworks display — "Ooh! Aah! Look what he's done now!." (TD).

One event might have served to warn the Republican establishment of what was about to happen, for in June 2014, an obscure college professor by the name of David Brat defeated Eric Cantor, the Republican Majority Leader in the House of Representatives. With the help of the Tea Party movement. Brat ran a campaign excoriating Cantor for being a tool of Wall Street and soft on illegal immigration. Trump, of course, would use the same kind of attacks against Hillary Clinton in the general election campaign in 2016.

Still, had Trump run against one attractive moderate conservative who could have united the anti-Trump forces from the beginning, he likely would never have won the nomination. In the vast majority of his primary victories, until very late, he amassed only roughly a third to forty percent of the vote, sometimes even less. The problem was that the remaining Republican primary field included at least five serious candidates, each of whom at the outset had legitimate aspirations.

Senator Marco Rubio of Florida presented himself as the attractive young face of the party, a conservative with Hispanic roots from a critical swing state; Chris Christie was the bulldog Governor of a blue state — no one doubted his fire or intelligence; Ted Cruz was the darling of conservative white evangelicals who had forced a government shutdown and gained many supporters as well as enemies for his trouble. John Kasich, the popular, fiscally conservative Governor of Ohio had a good story to tell, particularly for centrists who might be drawn to his established willingness to work across party lines. And then there was Jeb Bush, the heir apparent, also from Florida, who seemed the perfect candidate to appeal to independents and even moderate Democrats who distrusted Hillary.

The Republicans had had so many candidates (17) that, for their first debate in August 2015, they had to stage two events. The warm-up featured the seven candidates whose chances were viewed favorably only by themselves and close family members. The major debate was for the more serious candidates and there were ten of them.

If Donald was lucky to face so many serious candidates, Hillary seemed not to be facing any serious opposition at all. In the first Democratic debate, only four hopefuls showed up. Three of them could have walked down the streets of most major cities without turning a single head. There was Jim Webb of Virginia, certainly the most conservative hopeful. He would drop out shortly after the first debate when nobody seemed the slightest bit interested in what he had to say, including the other candidates. He would eventually announce that he did not plan to vote for Hillary, though he never specifically endorsed Trump and may not have voted for him. Then there was Martin O'Malley, the Governor of Maryland: competent, centrist, and having as much charisma as the back of a spoon.

Finally, there was Bernie Sanders. He wasn't even a Democrat caucusing with them mainly to have people to talk to. Of course, as it turned out, he did become a serious threat to the Clinton candidacy, a tribute to three things: first, he represented the growing progressive base of the party without competition from others, like Senator Elizabeth Warren of Massachusetts, who might have posed an even greater threat to Hillary; second, he became the only real alternative to the many in the party who simply disliked and distrusted Hillary; and third, he proved a formidable campaigner: his white hair and gravelly voice suggesting a biblical seriousness young people found hard to resist. Nobody could doubt his sincerity or that he was a man of genuine conviction, which came across in stark contrast to a candidate whose perceived lack of authenticity would prove perhaps her greatest weakness.

The Republicans, the first to hold their national convention, gathered in Cleveland, Ohio without the presence of President George W. Bush, Governor Mitt Romney, or Senator McCain. The only serious question was whether Trump would begin to execute the pivot to the middle supposedly necessary to secure the vital votes of independents and moderates. Trump did no such thing, instead doubling down in his acceptance speech on all the themes of his primary campaign and offering a very dark vision of the non-Trumpian past, a past that he insisted only he could rectify.

Hillary's acceptance speech, by contrast, struck an entirely different note. Yes, we had problems that needed attention but the Obama years had been good years for America and she would continue them. Her speech brimmed with optimism and what we could accomplish together. It was as if she had channeled her inner Reagan. Trump was dismissed as the dark shadow hovering overhead who sought to send us back to the worst parts of our past. In contrast to the G.O.P. Convention, the two most recent Democratic Presidents, Bill Clinton and Barack Obama, both gave strong, well-received speeches on Hillary's behalf. There was no question which candidate had had the better Convention, the post-convention polls all agreeing that Clinton had received a significant bounce.

That wasn't the only thing for Trump to worry about. By mid-August, some of the most respected elders of the Republican establishment had declared for Clinton, including former Michigan Governor William Milliken, former Deputy Secretary of Defense (under Ronald Reagan) Richard Armitage, former EPA Director (under George H.W. Bush) Frank Reilly, former South Dakota U.S. Senator Larry Pressler and former National Security Adviser to George H.W. Bush, Brent Scowcroft. And then there were the fifty former national security advisers to Republican Presidents from Nixon to George W. Bush who on August 8 had announced that they would not vote for Donald Trump, declaring him unfit to be Commander in Chief and saying that he would be "the most reckless president in American history."

Most politicians at this point might have been tempted to finally tack to the middle. That was certainly the kind of counsel Trump was receiving from key advisers like his campaign manager Paul Manafort and Reince Priebus, then Chairman of the Republican National Committee.

But Trump did the opposite, and with his decision to hire Steve Bannon, the campaign really began.

August 17 to August 31

On August 17, Trump delivered a bombshell, hiring Steve Bannon, Chairman of Breitbart News, to be the chief executive of the Trump campaign. William Kristol called it "the merger of the Trump campaign with the kooky right." It would prove to be the most important strategic choice of the campaign, for Bannon above all was insistent that Trump not let up for a second with his assault on Clinton, advice that obviously appealed to Trump's natural instincts. Bannon's elevation was also a reward of sorts, for during the nomination battle Breitbart News had become a virtual house organ of the Trump campaign, denigrating Trump's GOP opponents and extolling Trump at every turn. It got so bad that it was reported that at least six Breitbart staffers quit the paper. The choice was also a real poke in the eye for Paul Ryan since Breitbart News had led the charge against Ryan in his recent primary fight.

Bannon had fallen in love with Trump from the moment his campaign began, and was "practically giddy" over Trump's anti-immigrant announcement speech. "A beast," Bannon had called him — in Bannon's lexicon the ultimate compliment. (JG 161). Joshua Green relates how, less than a month later, Bannon arranged for Local 2455, the Border Patrol union in Laredo, Texas to invite Trump to the southern border. Trump came in late July notwithstanding that the national union had forced the Local to rescind the invitation. The visit, in Green's words, was "sheer pandemonium," highlighted by Trump's police-escorted motorcade to the World Trade Bridge. "The trip's purpose was pure theater" intending to make clear that Trump was serious about building the wall.

As important as the Bannon hire was, just as significant was the simultaneous naming of Kellyanne Conway as his campaign manager. Paul Manafort, whom Conway replaced, was briefly promoted to chief campaign strategist where he lingered a few days before being allowed to resign. From then on, Conway and Bannon would be, along with his family, Trump's closest advisers

As the campaign began, the candidates clearly had different priorities. Trump was campaigning hard for votes, holding large enthusiastic rallies and Hillary was campaigning hard for dollars, attending numerous fund-raisers in places like Martha's Vineyard, Nantucket, and the Hamptons.

Over the next few weeks, Hillary would raise more than $50 million in campaign contributions. At the same time, she would begin to lose almost all the momentum she had built up after the Convention.

After the election, Kellyanne Conway had this to say about those first few weeks:

> ...if everybody goes back and looks at the August travel schedules and the event schedule for Hillary Clinton and Donald Trump, that's the tale of the tape. See what happened in August, where you got a great bump out of the convention. You had a wildly popular president, wildly popular First Lady — much more popular than your candidate... She got a good bump but then she almost disappeared... It was remarkable to me *(Institute 194)*.

Trump wasn't just holding many more rallies than Clinton. He was also beginning his attack through the airwaves. His first ad, appearing August 20, described Hillary Clinton's America. It wasn't a place you'd want to visit, much less live. The ad began with images of handcuffed criminals and crowds of refugees. Then the deep voiced narrator intoned, "In Hillary Clinton's America, the system stays rigged against Americans. Syrian refugees flood in. Illegal immigrants convicted of committing crimes get to stay collecting social security benefits, skipping the line. Our borders open. More of the same. It's worse." But then we are reassured: "Donald Trump's America is secure. Terrorists and dangerous criminals kept out. The border secure. Our families safe. Change that makes America safe again. Donald Trump for President." Notice that phrase "skipping the line." If there was a general theme to Trump's standard stump speech it was how unfair everything had become under both the Democrats and

Republicans. For his most fixated supporters, unfairness wasn't about just one thing. It was about everything.

Notwithstanding Trump's dark vision, one place that still seemed pretty safe was the Iowa State Fair. Mike Pence spent two and a half hours visiting there on August 20, having a grand time with nary a terrorist in sight. He walked the Grand Concourse, carefully preserving his neutrality on the beef versus pork chop desirability question, happily sampling both. When asked how he liked the pork chop, he simply lofted the chop high over his head as if somebody was trying to steal it from him.

According to the Des Moines *Register*, he did get one other tough question: standing before the famed Butter Cow, Pence was asked how the festivities compared to the fair in his home state of Indiana, where he happened to be governor. "It's butter," he replied with a grin. In what might have been a Trumpian moment, he did claim that visiting the Iowa State Fair had always been on his bucket list — it just took Donald Trump to get him there. Pence had originally supported Ted Cruz but Trump knew that in swing states like Iowa, with its strong evangelical population, Pence would prove invaluable.

On August 31, Trump shocked virtually everyone when he went to Mexico for a private meeting with President Enrique Peña-Nieto. Nieto had invited both Clinton and Trump, expecting neither to accept. But Trump saw an opportunity and it worked. The all-important visuals for Trump following the meeting could not have been better for him. There he was, side by side with a foreign head of state looking and acting, it couldn't be denied, very presidential. Now people could really imagine him in the White House and be reassured. He said all the right things and President Nieto reciprocated, commenting "I am certain that he [Trump] has a genuine interest in building a relationship that would lead us to provide better conditions for our people." The visit was bold, decisive, a calculated risk that could have ended in disaster if Nieto had decided to show him up.

A few days later Trump made a stop at a place almost as foreign for him as Mexico: North Philadelphia. First, he met with a small group of Black business owners and community leaders. Then came the visuals, always the visuals: a brief emotional event in which Sheila Hightower, a Black woman, recounted how her twenty year old daughter was murdered by three men, two of them being undocumented immigrants. When Trump asked what happened to the men, she responded that they all received life sentences. "But they should have never been here" Trump helpfully added.

Next day, while Hillary was seeking to part the wealthy from a little more of their money, Trump was in Detroit at a Black church. The purpose wasn't to raise money. It was to reduce by one or two percent the overwhelming support Hillary enjoyed in the Black community. Why? In a close race in Michigan or Pennsylvania, shaving a point or two from Hillary's margin in the Black community could make all the difference.

Still, the mood amongst the Republican establishment was not optimistic. In late August, *The New York Times* reported that Republicans leaders were worried that if Trump lost by more than 5 points in swing states, it might cost them the Senate and at a minimum cut substantially into their majority in the House of Representatives. In some way, the pessimism seemed unfounded, for at virtually the same time a Pew Research poll showed Trump behind nationally by only four points, just outside the margin of error.

Meanwhile, Clinton did manage to interrupt her money-raising efforts on August 23 to unveil her small business plan. It included creating a standard deduction for the smallest businesses (cutting down on much paperwork), cutting red tape for community banks and credit unions (facilitating small business financing), and allowing small businesses to use cash (instead of accrual) accounting — eliminating a big headache for them. As Rhonda Abrams of the *Green Bay Press Gazette* wrote, "Clinton's proposals may not make you salivate with excitement, but they show that she understands some of the problems and realities of running a small business." Like so much of what Clinton proposed, it was thoughtful and comprehensive and also, unfortunately, entirely unnoticed.

Just a couple of days later, Clinton toggled back to focusing on Trump, arguing in Reno, Nevada that the support Trump was receiving from the fringe right was no accident. This, of course, was the kind of attack the media loved and it certainly was not ignored. "From the start," Clinton began, "Donald Trump has built his campaign on prejudice and paranoia." In evidence, she cited, among other things: Trump's initial refusal to disavow the support of former Ku Klux Klan leader David Duke; his description of Mexican immigrants as rapists and criminals; his insistence that thousands of Muslims celebrated on the streets of Jersey City after the 9/11 attacks; and his appearance on Alex Jones's show (who has questioned whether the Sandy Hook Massacre actually happened), telling Jones, "You have an amazing reputation." She also cited Trump's accusation that Ted Cruz's father had been involved in the assassination of John Kennedy, his leading role in questioning President Obama's citizenship even after the President produced a copy of his birth certificate, and his comment that a judge of Mexican heritage could not perform his duties impartially.

It was a brief compilation of Trump's greatest hits. Hillary then turned to Trump's hiring of Steve Bannon, citing the old Mexican proverb, "Tell me with whom you walk and I will tell you who you are," and concluding, "He's taking hate groups mainstream and helping a radical fringe take over one of America's two major political parties." She concluded:

> A man with a long history of racial discrimination, who traffics in dark conspiracy theories drawn from the pages of supermarket tabloids and the far reaches of the internet, should never run our government or command our military. He says he wants to *Make America Great Again*, but his real message remains [to] make America hate again.

August closed with Clinton speaking to the American Legion National Convention in Cincinnati, Ohio. Older white men were not her natural constituency. Yet she was able to cite the letter mentioned above of the fifty former Republican national security officials – most of them also older white guys – warning that Trump "would put at risk our country's national security and well-being." Building on the letter, Clinton asserted that "this election shouldn't be about ideology. It's not just about differences in policy. It truly is about who has the experience and the temperament to serve as president and commander in chief." It was an adroit speech, emphasizing her biggest edge over Trump in voters' minds: temperament.

Meanwhile, Trump traveled to Phoenix, Arizona introducing his ten-point immigration program at another packed rally. He began:

> While there are many illegal immigrants in our country who are good people, many, many, this doesn't change the fact that most illegal immigrants are lower skilled workers

with less education, who compete directly against vulnerable American workers, and that these illegal workers draw much more out from the system than they can ever possibly pay back. And they're hurting a lot of people that cannot get jobs under any circumstances.

Certainly, there was nothing overtly racist in those words. Trump then began drawing the stark contrast between himself and Hillary Clinton. Trump was for strict enforcement of the immigration laws, and she, according to him, worried much more about the illegal immigrants themselves than the American worker, "talking constantly about her fears that families will be separated, but she's not talking about the American families who have been permanently separated from their loved ones because of a preventable homicide, because of a preventable death, because of murder." Then Trump claimed that "while Hillary Clinton meets only with donors and lobbyists, my plan was crafted with the input of federal immigration officers, very great people. Among the top immigration experts anywhere in this country, who represent workers, not corporations, [this is] very important to us."

Trump's ten-point program made no concessions to anyone looking for a more generous immigration policy. It called for, among other things, the building of a wall along the U.S.-Mexico border and the issuance of "detainers for illegal immigrants who are arrested for any crime whatsoever" and their placement "into immediate removal proceedings, if we even have to do that." The speech, not surprisingly, was filled with many assertions that were simply untrue – for example, a claim that Hillary wanted to bring 620,000 Syrian refugees into the country when she actually had proposed accepting 65,000 in the year 2016 and had indicated no further position. Trump also claimed that Clinton and President Obama "support the release of dangerous, dangerous, dangerous criminals from detention" when Obama had made deporting serious criminals the focus of his deportation policy.

September 1 to September 25

Through early September each candidate continued to focus their attention on the other. In Florida on September 5, Clinton put the spotlight on a $25,000 donation that Trump had made to the campaign of the then Florida Attorney General Pam Bondi who was investigating Trump University. "The list goes on and on," she added noting "the scams, the frauds, the questionable relation-ships, the business activities that stiffed workers." She also called again for Trump to release his tax returns.

Meanwhile, Trump, in an interview with ABC, claimed, "Well, I just don't think she has a presidential look, and you need a presidential look." In Virginia Beach, he said "you know, Hillary likes to play tough with Russia" but "Putin looks at her and he laughs. Boy would he like to see her. That would be easy, because look at her deci-sions." In a speech at the Union League of Philadelphia before an invited audience of supporters, Trump attacked Hillary as dangerously trigger-happy. "Sometimes," he said, "it seemed like there wasn't a country in the Middle East that Hillary Clinton didn't want to invade, intervene in, or topple." He also pledged a huge increase in defense spending: a 60,000 increase in the current size of the Army of 540,000, 77 more ships for the Navy (raising its total fleet to 350), 13 more battalions for the Marines raising the total to 36, and an enlarged air force.

Tax returns also were prominently discussed in early September. By September 9, all of the other candidates had released theirs but Trump persisted in his refusal to do so. Though three-quarters of national poll respondents said that Trump should release his returns, he didn't seem to be paying a big political price in terms of erosion of voter support.

The other three returns told an interesting tale. From the Clintons' standpoint, the Pences might as well have been on food stamps. Their 2015 return showed that Pence and his wife Karen, a self-employed artist, had an adjusted gross income of $113,026 mostly from his gubernatorial salary, paying $8,956 in federal income tax. With the Clintons, however, we clearly entered the realm of the 1%. Their 2015 federal tax return showed that they made $10,594,529, paying federal income tax of $3,624,555 or to put it another way, the Clinton tax bill was more than 30 times the Pences' gross income. Actually, 2015 was a relatively bad year for the Clintons; they had made roughly $28 million in 2014. In between the two couples came the Kaines, their joint 2015 income of $313,441 on which they paid $63,626 in federal income tax placing them comfortably but not ostentatiously in the upper middle-class.

Then, on September 11, the first unscripted moment in the campaign occurred when Hillary had to leave abruptly from a 9/11 tribute at Ground Zero in New York City. It was all somewhat confusing because ninety minutes later, as she left Chelsea's apartment in the Flatiron District, she posed for pictures and said she felt great. Later it came out that she had been diagnosed with pneumonia on Friday the ninth but thought she could continue campaigning. The fact that she didn't disclose it right away raised new concerns about her penchant for secrecy.

Even more serious in terms of its lasting impact was the revelation of a statement she had made that same Friday at a fundraiser:

> You could put half of Trump's supporters in what I call a basket of deplorables. Right? The racist, sexist, homophobic, xenophobic, Islamophobic – you name it. And unfortunately there are people like that. And he has lifted them up. He has given voice to their websites that used to have only 11,000 people – now have 11 million.

Clinton almost immediately apologized for the remark but the damage was done. From then on, tee shirt makers would make lots of money at Trump rallies hawking items imprinted with slogans like "I'm an Adorable Deplorable."

Meanwhile, Donald Trump was still intent on burnishing his conservative credentials, unveiling a new tax plan at the Economic Club of New York that called for reducing taxes by $4.4 trillion over the next 10 years. He promised his plan would produce a 3.5% growth rate and 25 million new jobs. He also claimed that the economic growth induced by the tax cuts would actually result only in a net $2.6 trillion loss in federal revenues.

At about the same time, Trump finally acknowledged that President Obama was born in the United States. This was an issue that Trump, almost alone, tried to keep alive even after the President released a copy of his birth certificate. It was also a position that first endeared Trump to the extreme right. Letting go of it must have been tough for him but, as always, he made the most of it, claiming that he was responsible for the President actually furnishing the necessary proof.

Lest anyone think, however, that he was going soft or sentimental, Trump also suggested at a rally in Miami, "I think her [Hillary's] bodyguards should drop all weapons. I think they should disarm immediately. Let's see what happens to her. Take their guns away, O.K. It'll be very dangerous."

Trump had hit a new low, but unlike Hillary's deplorable comment the press treated it as just another moment of Donald being Donald. Trump, when questioned about the statement, simply said that he was trying to make a point about the importance of the Second Amendment to the U.S. Constitution. But what point? That Hillary should pack her own heat given the inevitable attempt on her life if the secret service disappeared? "Let's see what happens to her" was both stupid and disgusting but he made no apology. and lost no ground in the polls.

The gun issue became one of the key ways in which Trump, the wealthy New York businessman, cemented his support with rural America. It was also one of the key themes in his television ads. One particularly effective one showed a woman's house being invaded by a robber as she slept comfortably in her room and the narrator warns "Don't let Hillary leave you protected with nothing but a phone." In a chapter entitled "Girl Gunpower" in their book *The Great Revolt*, the authors devote a chapter to explaining exactly how potent this message was for many women in rural America who valued their gun rights.

I was not surprised. In the late sixties, I was traveling across the country in a Trailways Bus. Somewhere between Des Moines and Omaha I found myself next to a lovely young girl of about sixteen who wanted to be a nun. She was somewhat amazed when I pulled out a matzoh from my travel bag – "Those are the biggest crackers I've ever seen" – but it was nothing compared to her shock when it turned out I had never fired a gun or rifle. She herself had been squirrel hunting for as long as she could remember.

One other issue surfaced close to the first debate. Recent shootings of Black men by white police officers had occurred in Tulsa, Oklahoma and Charlotte, North Carolina once again raising the question of institutional racism in police departments around the country. For Hillary Clinton it was a problem that needed to be squarely faced. For Mike Pence, there was too much talk of institutional racism, which he dismissed as the "rhetoric of division." Police, Pence added, "are not a force for racism in America, they are a force for good. They stand for our families, they protect our homes, and they deserve our support and respect." The political positioning was all too obvious: Republicans needed to be seen as allies of the police, and the Democrats as sensitive to the perceptions in the minority communities.

The federal government does not actually compile statistics or keep a database on fatal police shootings but interestingly in 2015 *The Washington Post* had begun to do so. In analyzing its data, The *Post* concluded that African Americans were two and a half times more likely than white Americans to be shot and killed by police officers. The statistics were even more striking when it came to unarmed people. Unarmed Black men represented 40% of the unarmed people shot and killed by police in 2015. Conservatives responded that these statistics merely reflected that there is more violence in the Black communities but independent researchers analyzed the *Post*'s data and concluded that "the only thing that was significant in predicting whether someone shot and killed by police was unarmed was whether or not they were Black." One observer concluded that "there is some sort of implicit bias going on" reflecting that "officers are perceiving a greater threat when encountered by unarmed Black citizens."

As the candidates approached the time of the first scheduled debate, a *New York Times* report described the Clinton campaign as "unnerved by the tightening presidential race." For one thing, it appeared that many young people might be moving toward one of the two most important third-party candidates: Libertarian former Governor Gary Johnson of New Mexico and Green Party candidate, Jill Stein of Massachusetts.

A *New York Times*/CBS News poll conducted between September 9 and September 13 had disquieting news for both candidates. Almost two-thirds of those polled regarded neither candidate as honest or trustworthy. Temperament remained Trump's Achilles heel. Less than a third of voters (31%) believed he had the right personality and temperament to be President while more than half (51%) believed that Hillary did. On the other hand, barely more than a third (36%) believed that Hillary could bring about real change in the way things are done in Washington while almost half (48%) thought that Trump could. Another disquieting finding for Hillary was a Gallup Poll showing that only 18% of Americans thought the Affordable Care Act had helped them.

Of course, it was highly questionable how much any of the polls could be believed given a Rasmussen Reports' survey showing Trump with 44% support among likely U.S. voters to 39% for Clinton while an NBC/*Wall Street Journal* poll released at about the same time showed Clinton with a six point lead.

Clearly, it was still a very fluid race. Was Hillary making the best use of her time? On September 22 *The New York Times* reported that since Labor Day Hillary had held a total of six public events in swing states, less than the number of fundraisers she had also attended there over the same time period.

One voter had already made up his mind even before the first debate. According to Kathleen Kennedy Townsend, Robert Kennedy's daughter and an ex-lieutenant governor of Maryland, the 92 year-old President George H.W. Bush would be voting for Hillary Clinton. A Bush spokesperson refused to either confirm or deny it, invoking Bush's right of privacy.

At the same time Trump did get one endorsement of his own when Ted Cruz announced he was voting for the man who had accused Cruz's father of possibly being involved in the Kennedy assassination. Ambition can be a demanding muse. Cruz gave two reasons for his support: He had pledged to support the nominee whomever it was and anyone, even Trump, whom Cruz had previously called a "sniveling coward" and a "pathological liar," was still preferable to Hillary.

The endorsement was undoubtedly motivated in part by Cruz's political needs in Texas. For one thing, two of Cruz's most prominent supporters financially, the Mercer family and Peter Thiel, were strong Trump backers. Also, at the Republican Convention, Cruz had been roundly booed when it became clear that he would not use the speech as an opportunity to endorse Trump. I'm sure he expected the booing. What he probably didn't expect was the anger in the Texas delegation over his non-endorsement. His belated endorsement of Trump would hopefully repair some of the damage

In fairness to Cruz, there was also a more principled thinking behind his endorsement. At the Harvard conference, Cruz's campaign manager, Ted Roe, explained how Cruz viewed the gulf between Democrats and Republicans as less great than the gulf between Washington D.C. and those that it governs. "So" in Roe's words, "he wanted to go with a wrecking ball attitude of taking it to the insiders, taking on the establishment" (Institute 22). He thought he was the best man to do it because he had actually done it. But as he later told a friend, the best message in the world would not suffice without a certain kind of charisma that he ruefully admitted he simply didn't have.

Two milestones occurred the day before the debate. Arnold Palmer died at the age of eighty-seven and eighty-eight year old Vince Scully announced his last game at Dodger Stadium after a career of sixty-seven years, a game that fittingly ended with a dramatic Dodger home run that clinched the Western Division for them. Both men are revered. Both candidates would have loved to have their approval ratings.

September 26: The First Debate

With the election looking very close, both candidates had much to gain and much to lose. Past debates have been influential if not decisive in a number of elections. John Kennedy's television performance in the first presidential debate in 1960 had assured many voters that, despite his youth, he was ready for the presidency. Twenty years later in 1980, Ronald Reagan's composure and sense of humor completely undermined President Carter's attempt to paint him as a dangerous radical. If strong performances could make a difference, so too could gaffes. President Ford shocked the nation with his apparent belief that Soviet troops were not stationed in Poland; President George H.W. Bush was caught on camera looking at his watch, an unfavorable contrast with then-Governor Clinton's gift for empathy; and Al Gore's constant sighing made the idea of spending four years with the guy a slightly unnerving prospect.

Nobody seemed to be expecting a great deal from either candidate. Lonna Atkinson, director of the Center for the Study of Voting, Elections, and Democracy, suggested that for Clinton, given her recent pneumonia, "it's important for her not to look ill." For Trump, she said, "He just has to not lose it." Translation: Clinton's fate was in the hands of her make-up artist and Trump's on taking just the right number of tranquilizers.

The media couldn't have hyped the event more if the candidates had foregone the usual debate format in favor of pistols and seconds. CNN, MSNBC, and Fox News all treated it as the Super Bowl, Olympics, heavyweight championship, and World Cup rolled into one. They outdid themselves in hyping their own coverage of the event as well. Would there have been this excitement if the Republican candidate were someone other than Donald Trump? It's hard to know but how Trump would behave and whether he could control himself were certainly the two questions figuring most prominently in the pre-debate chatter. As it turned out the answers were badly and no.

He did manage to avoid beheading Hillary but it wasn't because by the end he didn't want to. He simply didn't have the energy. By that point, he had been so busy trying to flail his way out of Hillary's traps, it was a miracle he could leave the stage under his own power. His constant interrupting of her just underscored his reputation as a bully who deeply disrespected women. Then after the debate Trump became perhaps the first candidate to ever wander into the spin room, certainly a congenial atmosphere for him. Maya Angelou once said something to the effect that people may forget what you say but they will never forget how you made them feel. And this is where the debate, I thought at the time, might make the biggest difference, for it was hard to imagine women, particularly middle-aged and older, not being discomfited by Trump's constant interruptions of Hillary and his overall tone.

Hillary, on the other hand, grew more and more relaxed and confident as the evening wore on, even allowing herself to engage in a kind of shoulder shimmy toward the end of the debate. Clinton also looked so good and had performed with such energy that Trump simply looked foolish when he tried to make an issue of her stamina, as he had been trying on the campaign trail ever since her bout with pneumonia.

Most importantly, the debate allowed Clinton to display her articulateness, deep knowledge of the issues, and overall competence. This was no accident. She had basically stopped campaigning on the Wednesday before Monday's debate, scheduling no events on Thursday, Friday and Sunday and attending only the opening of the National Museum of African-American History in Washington, D.C. that Saturday.

Her debate prep sessions had been arduous. Clinton herself reports, "We would gather at noon and work late into the evening" (HC 104). But, for Clinton, they were perhaps a relief. She might have even preferred them to campaigning. After all, she was basically treating the debate like a final exam and she regularly aced those. In her memoir, she writes that she entered into the first debate with great confidence. Why? "In the end," she writes, "thanks to our practice sessions, I felt the deep sense of confidence that comes with rigorous preparation" (HC 107).

Both candidates entered the debate with confidence, one because of her extensive preparation, the other because he felt he didn't really need it at all. When asked about Hillary's debate preparation, Trump responded, "I don't need to rehearse being human."

The one group that was more than satisfied with Trump's performance were those already completely committed to him, at least in Coventry Township, Ohio. That's where the

Akron Beacon Journal sent one of its reporters to attend a Republican watch party for the debate at an establishment called the On Tap Grille & Bar. About fifty white Ohio Republicans of varying ages were in attendance. The debate did not seem to arouse much emotion either way. "Compared to different debates, this is boring," declared the chairman of the Summit County Young Republicans, certainly an accurate assessment given all the anatomical references in the party's pre-convention debates. Still, the Summit County Republican Party Chairman, Bryan Williams, found Trump's performance so overwhelming that "this is probably the last night of her campaign." Williams loved how Trump "forcefully stuck to positions he's had throughout the campaign."

In retrospect, Clinton may have been ill served by her preparation in one important respect. In her memoir, Clinton wrote: "In debate prep, I practiced keeping my cool while my staff fired hard questions at me. They'd misrepresent my record. They'd impugn my character. Sometimes I'd snap back and feel better for getting it off my chest. I'd think to myself 'now that I've done that here, I don't have to do it on live TV' It worked" (HC 104). But did it work too well? If somebody impugns your character as Trump was doing, actually making it the centerpiece of his campaign, what's wrong with showing a little emotion. True, she didn't want to appear hysterical, falling into a female stereotype, but there are degrees of emotional display below going bonkers that would, I believe, have served her well.

Trump once told *New York* magazine, "Women, you have to treat them like shit" (RP 162). Would a direct quote — there were others she could have chosen — at an opportune moment in the debate not turned the focus off her and on him? Yes, using *shit* in a television debate would have been a first, but it was his word, not hers.

September 27 to October 6

The first debate might not have gone as Trump had hoped but then again maybe it did. The first night after the debate, the Trump campaign, according to its finance chairman, raised $18 million through a combination of small and more traditional donors. This was on top of the more than $150 million dollars already laid away by the Trump campaign for a major advertising blitz.

Following the debate, Hillary gave a detailed speech pledging a renewed commitment to the idea of national service. It was rich in specifics. She wanted to triple the size of AmeriCorps, double the college scholarships that AmeriCorps members could earn through their service, and start a program to forgive student loans for those who serve. She also wanted to "grow the Peace Corps" and create "a National Service Reserve" which would give people an opportunity to serve their communities on less than a full-time basis. These were precisely the kind of thoughtful ideas that I hoped would shape her presidency.

As far as most of the media was concerned, however, she might as well have given the speech in a broom closet. The much bigger news that day was a POLITICO disclosed news clip showing Hillary in an unflattering light. It depicted her slightly mocking Sanders young supporters as "children of the great recession living in their parents basement" who just have "a deep desire to believe that we can have free college, free healthcare, that what we've done hasn't gone far enough, and that we just need to, you know, go as far as, you know, Scandinavia, whatever that means, and half the people don't know what that means, but it's something they deeply feel." Perhaps Hillary had only herself to blame, but really, which was more important: a little misguided attempt at humorous hyperbole at a private fund-raiser or a major proposal that could have changed a lot of lives had she become President.

The jousting continued.

Clinton, campaigning in Toledo, Ohio, railed against Trump as a cold-hearted businessman whose failure to pay taxes showed a complete lack of any sense of social responsibility:

> He has contributed nothing to our economy, nothing for Pell grants, nothing for veterans, nothing for the military. Trump represents the same rigged system that he claims he's going to change. Trump was taking from America with both hands and leaving the rest of us with the bill.

She also called for a law requiring major party presidential candidates to release their tax returns. Trump did his best to deflect the issue: "The unfairness of the tax laws," he said at a Pueblo, Colorado rally, "is unbelievable. It's something I've been talking about for a long time, despite, frankly, being a big beneficiary of the laws. But I'm working for you now. I'm not working for Trump."

Meanwhile, Bill Clinton was doing his best to help Hillary. Sometimes, however, it seemed he might be helping Trump more than his wife. On October 4, he called Obamacare "the craziest thing in the world" because "the people who are out there busting it, sometimes 60 hours a week, sometimes end up with their premiums doubled and their coverage cut in half." It was a remark the media and the Trump campaign immediately seized upon.

At the same time, however, Bill was, in his own way, addressing her key vulnerability, the idea that she was just more of the same at a time when the public was anything but happy with the status quo. At a rally in Flint, Michigan

— the same rally where he made the Obamacare gaffe — Clinton also acknowledged that the election was being driven by "legitimate road rage over economic stagnation and the temptation to vote for someone who is entertaining." He added, "This is a change election. The question is — what kind of change do we want?" He wanted to give voters positive reasons for backing Hillary like tougher financial regulation, debt-free college, and universal pre-school. Bill in fact was talking about change more personally and directly than Hillary herself and focusing on the future with greater clarity. Even he, however, was focusing on the economy, not perhaps fully understanding the cultural chasm that separated her from so many Trump supporters.

Still, Hillary's cautious, no unforced errors campaign seemed to be working, polls showing her with substantial leads in Michigan and Pennsylvania, two key states in the Blue Wall intended to guarantee her victory, though she trailed in Ohio (not part of the Blue Wall).

The polls were one thing but it was still hard to ignore the excitement Trump was creating at his rallies.

In retrospect, an early October rally held at the Prescott Valley Event Center in Prescott, Arizona explains a good deal about Trump's ultimate success. The Arizona *Republic* headline the next day read "Rally electrifies deep-red Prescott Valley." Before an adoring crowd, Trump castigated Hillary and Obama and made fun of Bill for his critical remarks on Obamacare ("I bet he went through hell last night"). Six thousand people were packed inside the arena with another ten to fifteen thousand, by police estimates, outside. Not surprisingly for an Arizona audience, he spent a lot of time talking about immigration — "We are going to build the wall. Ok are you ready? Who's going to pay for it?" To which crowd gleefully responded, "Mexico."

The four reporters covering the event for the *Republic* – it did not take four reporters to cover Clinton rallies, usually one would do — described how "Trump devoted considerable time to noting incidents in which undocumented immigrants were either accused of murder or other serious crimes." At the same time, he never lost sight of what many wanted most of all: "Our economic agenda is very, very simple," he declared at one point, "jobs, jobs, jobs." He had absorbed Bill Clinton's 1992 campaign mantra, "It's the Economy, Stupid" better than Hillary herself.

Trump was not the only one expressing himself at his rallies. Women sported tee shirts, emblazoned with "Adorable Deplorable" while Trump baseball caps with "Make America Great Again" were everywhere. A major Trump rally often also came with a certain amount of tension, inevitably drawing protestors and requiring a police presence to keep protestors and Trump supporters at a distance. The Prescott rally was no different but the major point was how Trump's assembled fans gave him rave reviews.

Reporters were doing their best to understand this phenomenon and rally attendees gave many different reasons for their devotion (repealing Obamacare, securing the borders, shaking up Washington). The most striking thing, however, was simply how much his fans just liked him and even saw themselves in him. One voter noted, "He's like we are, except he's extremely rich." and another said, "He really is one of us. He is for the country. He loves the country." And a former Cruz supporter, now solidly behind Trump, admitted "he's kind of grown on me."

Many attendees cited his belief in *America first*. One voter noted, "I think it's nonsense we are helping Syrian refugees and we have Americans here that are starving. What about Americans that pay tax dollars? Why aren't we taken care of?" Another declared, "I feel like too long, we've been the kind of the country that's taking care of everybody but ourselves... we're worrying too much about other people when we should be worrying about ourselves."

On October 5, the vice-presidential candidates had their debate. Given the tone of the campaign, part of it was all too predictable. Kaine accused Trump of having "his personal Mount Rushmore: Vladimir Putin, Kim Jong-Un, Muammar Gaddafi and Saddam Hussein." He then highlighted some of Trump's biggest hits insult-wise. Pence countered that none of his insults matched Hillary's statement on deplorables. It was not an easy debate to score but the consensus seemed to be that Pence had done a little better. I'm not sure what "a little better" meant. That Pence came out looking more vice-presidential?

Tim Kaine, a civil rights lawyer before moving into politics, had home court advantage since the debate was held in Farmville, Virginia, a locale that had been a center of the civil rights struggle in Virginia. The debate would affect the campaign not one iota. There were no serious gaffes; neither man appeared in sequins or silk pajamas; both knew that Aleppo was a Syrian city, not a new dog food. They each defended their respective bosses in their own way.

The most memorable moments, frankly the most honest and revealing of themselves, occurred when the two candidates discussed social issues. Pence, if you read between the lines, came very close to admitting that he believed that all abortions should be simply outlawed on moral grounds, not just left to the states to decide; Kaine acknowledged that as a Catholic he was deeply troubled, given his personal opposition to capital punishment, by allowing executions to go forward while he was Governor of Virginia.

Then, two days after the debate came the bombshell that it was difficult to imagine even a Donald Trump surviving.

October 7 to October 19

The "fatal" bullet had come courtesy of *The Washington Post*'s disclosure of the tape of a conversation that Donald Trump had had with one-time *Today* show host Billy Bush in 2005. To call it lewd is an understatement. It showed Trump bragging in the most vulgar terms how fame enables him to grope beautiful women and seek sex with them. At one point, he describes in graphic detail how he unsuccessfully sought to bed one woman, even offering to help her buy furniture. The most cringe-worthy moment in the tape came when Trump claimed "when you're a star, they let you do anything. Grab them by the pussy. You can do anything."

Until the tape, only one Republican Congressman had refused to endorse Trump. It appeared that number would now grow substantially as Speaker Paul Ryan immediately disinvited Trump from an event in Wisconsin where they had been scheduled to appear together that night.

The Republican National Committee, led by Reince Priebus, now faced an important question. Did they want to give up on the presidential race altogether and concentrate on holding on to the Senate and protecting their majority as much as possible in the House? If they did, then the Committee would simply opt out of its joint agreement with the Trump campaign and concentrate all its resources elsewhere. Ultimately, Priebus decided to stay with Trump, likely the key unsung moment in the campaign given all the organizational and informational support that the RNC was giving him. Trump's key advisers subsequently acknowledged that Trump could not have won without that support.

Trump responded to the tape by releasing a short video statement that was vintage Trump, briefly apologizing for his words and then launching into a wholesale attack on Bill Clinton, claiming that Clinton said and did much worse and that Hillary Clinton intimidated his victims. He also asserted that the remarks certainly didn't reflect the man he is now.

Ironically, the Billy Bush tape served Trump in one important respect for it cast aside what could have eventually been an even bigger story that had been breaking just an hour or so earlier than *The Washington Post* revelation: the announcement by the Department of Homeland Security and the Office of the Director of National Intelligence that the Russian government was behind the hacking of the Democratic National Committee emails. Moreover, just a half- hour after the *Post* story broke, WikiLeaks released the first group of emails that Russia had hacked from the account of John Podesta, Clinton's Campaign Director. As Kathleen Jamieson describes in her engrossing and important book *Cyber-War: How Russian Hackers and Trolls Helped Elect a President*, the Sunday morning talk shows, faced with the need to allot time among three major stories, ended up "sidetracking the declaration that the Russians were behind the hacking and counterbalancing the Access Hollywood disclosures with supposed revelations from the leaked Clinton speeches...." And, she adds, "In the subsequent news coverage and in the final two debates, the illegal Russian provenance of the stolen content was all but ignored by journalists" (KJ 160). It was a minor miracle for the Trump campaign.

The fall-out from the Billy Bush tape, however, continued. Senator Kelly Ayotte of New Hampshire, engaged in a tight race for re-election, Senator McCain of Arizona, and Representative Joe Heck of Nevada who was running for an open Senate seat in Nevada, all were reported as having withdrawn their support for Trump.

Then Senator Susan Collins announced in *The Washington Post* that she would not be voting for Trump either, writing: "This is not a decision I make lightly for I am a lifelong Republican. But Donald Trump does not reflect historical Republican values nor the inclusive approach to governing that is critical to healing the divisions in our country." Carly Fiorina — the candidate whose face Trump had ridiculed — called on Trump to step aside in favor of Mike Pence, saying Trump "no longer represents me or my party." She remained adamant, however, in her opposition to Secretary Clinton whom she described as "unfit to be President" and who must be defeated "for the sake of our Constitution and the rule of law."

Still, despite the defections, there had not been a wholesale disavowal of Trump's candidacy. State party chairs were not calling for his withdrawal and while Mitt Romney continued in his refusal to endorse Trump, Romney's niece, Ronna Romney McDaniel, the Michigan Republican Party Chairwoman, while asserting that he must "apologize over and over again" for his remarks, made clear that she was still behind him.

With the second debate coming up, many seemed to be adopting a wait and see attitude. It would prove a turning point in the election, allowing Trump to go on the offensive and deflect at least some of the attention away from the tape. One thing was clear. Donald Trump would not go gently into that good night.

The Detroit *Free Press* succinctly captured what happened at the second debate with its headline: Nothing off-limits for Clinton-Trump. And there wasn't. Even before it began, Trump held a news conference with three women, one of whom said point blank "Mr. Trump may have said some bad words but Bill Clinton raped me and Hillary Clinton threatened me."

At one point during the debate, Trump looked directly at Clinton and advised her that if elected he would appoint a special prosecutor to investigate her. It was extraordinary — the first time that one presidential candidate had ever threatened to jail another. Later, legal experts pointed out that the President does not have the power to appoint a special prosecutor. Indeed, the President does not even have the legal authority to force his or her Attorney General to sue or prosecute any individual – something that Trump would learn well into his presidency when he wanted to request the Department of Justice to investigate Hillary.

Trump apologized again for the Billy Bush tape, explaining it was "locker room banter," that occurred long ago. He repeated that the tape did not represent who he is now. Clinton responded, "It is clear to anyone who heard it, it represents exactly who he is." Trump again took the offensive, citing how Bill Clinton was "abusive to women" and accusing Hillary of being an enabler who "bullied, attacked, shamed, and intimidated" Bill's victims. Hillary's riposte was simply to remind herself of Michelle Obama's advice, "When they go low, you go high." It was an anemic response. Indeed, the second debate provided one of those moments where Clinton's need to be the adult in the room and not show anger in my view disserved her. When your opponent says that if he were President you'd be in jail and adds later "she has hate in her heart" you should take it personally and respond with a few choice words. But as one writer has described, "Clinton decided not to rise to the bait. While she was critical of Trump she did not match Trump's seething anger in kind" (MG 70).

Could the candidates say anything positive about each other? That was actually the last question from the audience in the town hall format.. Clinton answered first and said how much she respected Donald's children and added that they reflected well on Trump. Trump said that he wasn't sure that Clinton's comment was meant as a compliment (even though it clearly was since she had mentioned that it reflected well on Donald), but then he launched into a sincere compliment of his own about how Clinton keeps fighting and never gives up. It wasn't actually a love fest but seemed briefly to alter the mood of the night enough to allow the pair to shake hands, something they hadn't done at the beginning of the debate, perhaps another first.

In spite of an overall better performance in the second debate, Trump was hardly out of the woods. The next day Paul Ryan let it be known that he would no longer campaign for nor defend Donald Trump's candidacy. He said he would concentrate on making sure that there was a strong House majority to defend against a Clinton presidency. Ryan's announcement would result in his name being booed at Trump rallies almost as loudly as the invocation of Secretary Clinton's name.

No liberal could have been fiercer in his or her denunciation of Donald Trump than some of his conservative critics. In his post-second debate column, George Will had this to say: "What did Donald Trump have left to lose Sunday night? His dignity? Please. What was his campaign theme? His Cleveland convention was a mini-Nuremberg rally for Republicans whose three-word recipe for making America great again was 'Lock her up.'" Then Will gave four reasons why he hoped Trump would stay in the race, including "…he will give the nation the pleasure of seeing him join the one cohort, of the many cohorts he disdains, that he most despises – 'losers.'"

Certainly, if newspaper endorsements were to decide the election, Hillary would win in a landslide. By mid-October, the Houston *Chronicle*, the Arizona *Republic*, the Dallas *Morning News*, the San Diego *Union-Tribune*, the

Richmond *Times-Dispatch*, and the Cincinnati *Enquirer*, all of which had endorsed Romney, had endorsed Clinton. The Cincinnati *Enquirer* and Arizona *Republic* hadn't endorsed a Democrat in their entire history, but for the *Enquirer* a Trump presidency would be "a clear and present danger to our country" while the *Republic* noted, "When the president of the United States speaks, the world expects substance. Not a blistering tweet."

Even some young partisans were turning against him. With the Billy Bush tape clearly in mind, the College Republicans at the University of New Mexico disavowed him because:

> The Oval Office is no place for a vulgar and classless individual. The leader of the free world is someone that young girls and boys from all over the country look to for leadership and maturity. The American President should be a role model, a leader, not someone who would bring shame and embarrassment to our country.

Hillary, however couldn't take too much comfort in their statement, for it also pronounced her as unfit to be President. Their solution: Vote for Gary Johnson, an endorsement that must have been especially pleasing to Johnson since he had been Governor of New Mexico from 1995 to 2003.

The timing of the second debate wasn't the only break Trump caught. On October 12, WikiLeaks released 2,000 more emails from John Podesta's hacked account. This was nothing decisive, but any change of topic was welcome news for the Trump campaign.

Trump seemed to be getting more desperate. As more women come forward to accuse him of sexual assault,

Trump responded by accusing Hillary of being on drugs during the last debate. Even Mike Pence wasn't quite willing to go along with that latest charge.

Trump's tweeting was also becoming more and more shrill. On the morning of October 15, at 6:51 AM he tweeted about the "100% fabricated and made up charges against me," and at 7:45 he tweeted "this election is being rigged by the media pushing false and unsubstantiated charges and outright lies in order to elect crooked Hillary." Finally, at 8:23, a final morning tweet read, "Hillary Clinton should have been prosecuted and should be in jail. Instead she is running for President in what looks like a rigged election." The rigged election theme was also becoming a staple of his political rallies. And he was getting support. Sharing the stage with Trump at a rally in Portsmouth, New Hampshire, Jeff Sessions charged, "They are attempting to rig this election."

In a clear attempt to limit the impact of Trump's remarks, Mike Pence, on Meet the Press, stated that he and Trump would "absolutely" accept the will of the American people and Rudy Giuliani and Pence, among others, attempted to interpret Trump's statements about a rigged election as simply a complaint about a biased media. Trump, however, sabotaged these clarifications when he tweeted that the election is being rigged "at many polling places. SAD." This last claim clearly had nothing to do with media bias and there was no evidence to support it.

Still, some surrogates charged ahead. Most notable was Newt Gingrich telling Fox News that in the primaries "Fourteen million people picked Donald Trump," but that now "twenty TV executives decided to destroy him." Then, in an exaggeration that might have made even Trump blush, Gingrich added: "Without the unending, one-sided assault of the news media, Trump would be beating Hillary Clinton by 15 points." Trump's rigging theme did find fertile soil with some of Trump's most devoted followers, with the Milwaukee County Sheriff, for example, tweeting: "It's incredible that our institutions of gov, WH, Congress, DOJ, and big media are corrupt & all we do is bitch. *Pitchforks and torches time* (my emphasis)."

It was left to Paul Ryan to be the adult not in need of supervision when, through a spokesperson, he declared "our democracy relies on confidence in election results, and the Speaker is fully confident the states will carry out this election with integrity." The Ohio Secretary of State agreed, pointing out that Democratic and Republican poll watchers observe the proceedings at each polling location, including the counting of votes, a process he correctly described as "completely open and transparent."

Little wonder that at a private fundraising event in Seattle, Hillary Clinton described the campaign as "incredibly painful" and hurting both "my country" and "our democracy," adding, "Damage is being done that we're going to have to repair. Divisions are being deepened that we're going to have to try and heal." Of course, implicit in these statements was the conviction that she would be the next President.

The Democrats were in fact feeling incredibly optimistic even allowing themselves, according to one *New York Times* article, that they might yet take the House of Representatives. (In the end, they would pick up only six seats still leaving them with a deficit of 241 to 194.

Meanwhile, President Obama was in Ohio scratching away at the idea that Trump was a friend of the workingman. "The guy spent 70 years on this earth showing no regard for working people...And then suddenly he's going to be the champion of working people. Come on. Come on, man." Though the President praised Hillary as "the most qualified woman ever to seek the Presidency" and "she's going to be great at it," most of his fire and passion was directed against Trump.

Amidst all this, on October 19, the third and final debate was held. Nothing new emerged to change the direction of the campaign. Trump managed to steer clear of the spin room and once again the consensus was that Hillary had won the debate. The CNN post-debate voter survey had Clinton winning the debate 51% to 39%. The post debate talking heads seemed to agree that Trump needed a game-changer given the polls, which now showed Clinton with a clear lead nationally and in most swing states. He didn't get it. Indeed, one CNN panelist read an email he received from a Republican congressman from Florida conceding that Trump was now "toast, toast, toast."

But there was one discordant note for Hillary. CNN's focus group of undecided Nevada voters watching the debate from the CNN studio was asked after the debate whether the debate had helped them make up their minds. Many said it had and by a more than 2 to 1 margin, they had moved toward Trump. Were the experts missing something? We would know in a few weeks.

October 20 to October 27

With the debates out of the way, the race was clearly in the home stretch. Things were looking very good for Hillary as the week began. An ABC/*Washington Post* tracking poll taken right after the last debate now showed her with a 12-point advantage over Trump — the previous poll had shown her ahead by four points — and Kellyanne Conway agreed in an interview, "We are behind." Even Texas seemed to be in play with one poll showing her behind by only three points and another showing her leading in Arizona by five. Still, the race was far from over with Trump actually leading by four points in the latest Ohio poll — a poll that should have made the Clinton campaign particularly uncomfortable since it suggested that blue wall states like Michigan and Wisconsin, even Pennsylvania, fitting the profile of Ohio might also be more in play than was then apparent. Other state polls showed Trump behind by only two points in Nevada and one point in North Carolina, very much within the margin of error.

Two columns might have also kept the Clinton team up at night had it known about them.

The first was a column by Kathleen Parker appearing in the *Tallahassee Democrat* who thought the race still extremely volatile. The volatility, she contended was provided by two groups of voters: The Dislikers and the Undecideds. They were not, in Parker's definitions, the same thing. The Dislikers "deeply dislike both candidates equally," the Undecideds," though not necessarily disliking the candidates, were "still waiting for a spark that will guide them to the Truth." The two groups together "form the Unknowables – this election's monstrous, unquantifiable X factor." Her bold prediction was that most of them "will fall for Trump – not because he's the better candidate but because nearly three-quarters of Americans think the country is galloping in the wrong direction, the usual remedy for which is to switch horses." Parker turned out to be more prescient than any of the talking heads one encountered on cable television night after night. In her campaign memoir, Hillary cited exit polls showing that 18% of the electorate had negative views of both she and Donald Trump and that this group broke for Trump 47% to 30%. The Dislikers went for Trump just as Parker predicted.

Ledyard King of the USA Today Network gave the second warning. Focusing on the key state of Florida. King suggested that Hillary was having a particularly difficult time bringing millennials (18 to 34 year olds) to her side. This was not to say that many were thinking of voting for Trump, but the third party candidates, Gary Johnson and Jill Stein, were seen by many as an attractive alternative. One Johnson supporter admitted to knowing very little about him, except that he wasn't one of the two major party candidates. That apparently was enough. Particularly troubling for Hillary's electoral prospects, King found, was her problems with former Sanders supporters put off by her well-compensated speeches to Wall Street and the relationship between the Clinton Foundation and the State Department. One young woman, who planned to vote for Stein, told King: "I think she's [Clinton] very much the pinnacle of the party system and all that's wrong in the country." Even Clinton's supporters hardly offered a ringing endorsement, one voting for her because she lied less often than Trump.

Interestingly, a companion article detailed the problems Trump was having with older voters in Sumter County, Florida where a small band of Republicans for Hillary had formed and where the support for Romney in 2012 was much broader than it seemed to be for Trump. The median age of Sumter County is 66.6. (It turned out that Clinton had much more to be worried about than Trump who actually did substantially better than Romney in Sumter County beating Hillary by more than 30,000 votes (52,722 to 22,631). Romney had won the county by 21,000 (40,646 to 19,524). Meanwhile Johnson and Stein combined for 273,000 votes in a state Trump carried by 121,000 votes.

Two events stand out from this brief period of the campaign, neither in any way pivotal but both worth recounting. On October 20, the day after the final debate, the two candidates appeared at the annual Al Smith charity fundraising dinner hosted by the Archdiocese of New York, a tradition of presidential elections for more than fifty years. It is supposed to be a night away from the campaign trail when the candidates engage in a little self-deprecating humor and perhaps point gentle fun in the direction of the opposing candidate. True to the spirit of the occasion, Clinton began by noting that she was taking a break from her "rigorous nap schedule" but most of the rest of her twenty-minute speech was aimed at Trump himself, none too gently. Trump responded in kind with a speech of almost equal length in which he too started off well enough, noting that modesty was "perhaps my best quality." Then, poking fun at himself and Melania, he noted how biased the media was against him but only for the purpose of setting up this quip: "You want the proof? Michelle Obama gives a speech, and everyone loves it. My wife, Melania, gives the exact same speech and people get on her case." He also poked fun at Hillary, at first in a kidding way: "It's great to be here with 1,000 wonderful people, or as I call it, a small intimate dinner with some friends. Or as Hillary calls it, her largest crowd of the season." But then Trump turned darker, accusing Hillary of hypocrisy and then calling Clinton "corrupt" adding she was in "public tonight, pretending not to hate Catholics," a remark that actually drew boos from the audience.

It was a sad night for those who remember different and better elections. I couldn't help but think of a time when Senator Goldwater and President Kennedy actually talked about going around the country together engaging in Lincoln-Douglas style debates if Goldwater got the Republican nomination in 1964. Goldwater did get the nomination, but by then President Kennedy was dead.

The other event, a speech to be delivered by Trump in Gettysburg, Pennsylvania, was supposed to reset the Trump campaign. The idea was to rollout a "Contract with the American Voters," a detailed accounting of what Trump intended to accomplish that would give both his base and more moderate Republicans something they could rally around. The beginning of the prepared text of the speech released to the press was pitch perfect. It began:

> I'm not a politician, and have never wanted to be one. But when I saw the trouble our country was in, I knew I couldn't stand by and watch any longer. Our country has been so good to me. I love our country. I felt I had to act.
>
> Change has to come from outside this broken system. The fact that the Washington establishment has tried so hard to stop our campaign is only more proof that our campaign represents the kind of change that only arrives once in a lifetime.
>
> I am asking the American people to rise above the noise and clutter of our broken politics, and to embrace that great faith and optimism that has always been the central ingredient of the American character. I am asking you to dream big.

It is hard to imagine three paragraphs more perfectly attuned to all of Trump's needs. It had a spirit of optimism and gratitude — two words one didn't easily associate with the candidate. The inspired phrase "the noise and clutter of our broken politics" could resonate with just about the entire country.

The rest of the text then described Trump's Contract. Trump's people had positioned him perfectly to restart his campaign.

So what did he do? Instead of sticking to the prepared text, he immediately veered off course in the worst possible way, pledging to sue after the election every woman who had accused him of sexual assault. Undoubtedly, his staff had never dreamed that his first promise to America would be to sue 11 different women. He had created the next day's headline in one minute and made the rest of his "Gettysburg Address" totally anti-climatic. *The Guardian* headline was nonetheless typical: "Trump uses Gettysburg Address to Threaten to Sue Assault Accusers."

October 27 to Election Day

Whether FBI Director Jim Comey's letter announcing the review of a new batch of Clinton emails resulted in giving the Presidency to Donald Trump will always be a matter of intense debate but it is uncontested that it changed the Clinton strategy for the final week and a half of the campaign. The original plan — to go high and talk about all she wanted to accomplish — gave way instead to a tactical decision to concentrate her fire on Trump himself. Whether that was a fatal mistake we will never know.

The day before Comey's letter, Trump had held a big rally at the Tallahassee Automobile Museum, part of a multi-city swing through Florida, including appearances in Naples, St. Augustine, Tampa, and Sanford. The State's capital is a Democratic stronghold but North Florida is not and the venue brought people in from across the region and southern Georgia. Trump continued to hammer away at Hillary calling her "as crooked as a three-dollar bill."

Trump also went to Miami where he spoke at a gathering of his own employees at the Miami golf course he owns. As part of the event, employees were invited to approach "Mr. Trump" and thank him for all he had done for them (the moment felt like something right out of *Brave New World*). During his brief remarks, Trump asserted that his employees were having a "terrible time" with Obamacare, referring specifically to the rise in premiums that are affecting the subsidized individual healthcare market created by the Act. In fact, most of his employees received their health insurance through their employer, as did 49% of all covered Americans in 2015, and were not part of the individual healthcare market. Still, the expected steep rise in premiums for 2017 in a few swing states, most notably Arizona, North Carolina, and Iowa, was definitely a worry for the Clinton campaign.

Meanwhile, Hillary was at Broward College urging her supporters not to get complacent, predicting "a close election.' She contrasted her views with Trump's on minimum wage, infrastructure investment and clean energy and also criticized Trump for his statement in their last debate that he "would keep people in suspense" as to whether he would accept the results of the election.

Then on Friday afternoon October 28 came the Comey letter. Addressed to the congressional committees investigating the Clinton emails, it simply informed them that additional emails had been discovered that might be pertinent to the use of Clinton's private server. It was being sent, a senior FBI official said, "out of an abundance of caution." The emails had been discovered on the computer of former Congressman Anthony Weiner, the estranged husband of one of Hillary's most important advisers, Huma Abedin. It was yet to be determined whether any were even relevant to or would require the re-opening of the investigation. Nevertheless, the FBI had completely upended the 2016 presidential race. John Podesta, Clinton's campaign manager, immediately called on the FBI to release additional information and expressed confidence that the new emails would not change the FBI's July findings.

Trump could not suppress his excitement at the news and it was heartwarming to see how quickly his faith in the system could be restored. He now admitted to his rallies that he may have been wrong in his initial criticism of the agency. Not surprisingly, Trump completely misrepresented what the FBI had done, making it seem as if it was practically a foregone conclusion that Clinton would be indicted when the FBI hadn't even decided that the emails contained anything new.

That night, the prognosticator Nate Silver told Lawrence O'Donnell that the impact of this development on the polls would not be known until the middle of the following week, particularly since a number of major survey organizations do not contact voters over the weekend.

After a muted response on Friday, the next day Hillary started fighting back. At a rally in Daytona Beach, Florida, she said, "It's pretty strange to put something like that out with such little information right before the election. In fact, it's not just strange: it's unprecedented and deeply troubling." John Podesta, her campaign manager was even stronger in his criticism: "By providing selective information, he has allowed partisans to distort and exaggerate to inflict maximum political damage. Comey has not been forthcoming with the facts."

As the final week of the campaign approached, many supporters on both sides saw the end of days if their candidate did not win. The most ardent Trump supporters seemed convinced that a Clinton presidency would spell the end of freedom of religion, that illegal immigrants would flood into every state, that the Second Amendment would be rendered a nullity, and that a grasping federal government would essentially take over the country. For Hillary's biggest fans, the only explanation for a vote for Trump was blatant racism or an IQ below 70. Trump's stoking of his voters' fears had been a key part of his playbook from the start but Hillary's new favorite line — "Friends don't let friends vote for Trump" — played on her own voters' fears.

Meanwhile, over the weekend, Trump was in Arizona for the seventh time in the campaign. The Arizona *Republic* reported that the Republican nominee "sounded his usual crowd-pleasing themes — promises to secure the border; build a wall, end a 'crime wave' caused by undocumented immigrants and end the 'catastrophe' of Obamacare." He also continued his relentless attack on Hillary, calling her email problems "the biggest political scandal since Watergate" and continuing his claim that "Hillary set up an illegal server for the obvious purpose of shielding her criminal conduct from public conduct and exposure."

It was perhaps fitting that the final full week of the campaign would begin on Halloween.

As the week began Trump seemed to be doubling down on his efforts to delegitimize, Hillary, accusing her of "selling" the office of Secretary of State during her time there and asserting she would do the same with the Oval Office if given the chance. He accused her of being the most corrupt person ever to run for the Presidency.

Echoing his theme, Trump supporters were promising to wreak havoc if the country had the nerve to prefer Clinton. E.J. Dionne noted, "The most depressing news from last week did not come from the presidential campaign. It came from Representative Jason Chaffetz, who told us a Republican Congress would be all about investigating a President Clinton." "We've got two years worth of material already lined up," Chaffetz said. This was the same Chaffetz to whom Comey's bombshell letter was addressed, a letter that Chaffetz immediately and inaccurately portrayed as saying that the Clinton case had been reopened.

Meanwhile, at a rally in Cincinnati, Hillary talked about "this new email story" and asked "why in the world" would "the FBI decide to jump into an election without any evidence of wrongdoing with just days to go." Then she went on:

> Look I've said repeatedly I made a mistake. I'm not making any excuses, but I will tell you this: if they want to look at more emails of one of my staffers, by all means, go ahead, look at them. And I know they will reach the same conclusion they reached when they looked at my emails last year. Right? It wasn't even a close call and I think most people have moved on.

It sounded defensive but what else could she say. Then she segued back to her major theme:

> Let's not get distracted from the real choice in this election. Donald Trump has proven himself to be temperamentally unfit and totally unqualified to be president and commander in chief... I have watched and known a lot of people who have run for president, both Republicans and Democrats. And look, I've had my disagreements with Republicans... but I never doubted their fitness to serve in this office.

Making the case for unfitness, Clinton also alluded to the 30 launch officers who had warned against Trump getting anywhere near the nuclear codes and encouraged voters to think about the "difference between electing a president who will do nothing and [a] president who will tackle the epidemic of gun violence in America." A little later, campaigning in Florida, Clinton noted that when a journalist told Trump that people were worried about how casually he talks about using nuclear weapons, he said, "Well, then, why are we making them." Almost her entire speech was devoted to replaying some of Donald's greatest hits: his belittling of John McCain's heroism, his attack on the Gold Star Khan family, his questioning Obama's citizenship, and his assertion that "I alone" can fix the country's problems. This was followed by a long attack on Trump's "demeaning, degrading, insulting and assaulting women" and what elevating such a man to the presidency would mean to the young girls of the nation.

As the electoral map came into sharper focus, one thing seemed clear. As John Cassidy pointed out in a short New Yorker piece asking "Why is Donald Trump in Michigan and Wisconsin?" Trump had to peel off a Blue State to win even if he ended up carrying North Carolina, Ohio, Nevada and Florida. It would not be easy. Neither Michigan nor Wisconsin nor Pennsylvania had voted for a Republican for President in twenty-eight years. Long odds to be sure but Nate Silver's Five Thirty-eight now saw a one in four chance for a Trump Presidency — right before the FBI letter it had been a one in ten chance.

As it turned out, John Cassidy was certainly asking the right question about Trump's presence in Wisconsin and Michigan. In *Shattered*, the authors report that Trump's internal polling actually showed him with a lead at about this point but the Trump campaign did not want to indicate that fact for fear that no one would believe them (JA 364-365). There was, of course, another good reason to keep quiet: why alert the Clinton campaign to the trouble they were in. Cassidy's article predicted with prescient accuracy what actually happened when he wrote:

The big challenge facing the Republican candidate is that, in recent elections, as many as half of all white working-class voters haven't voted at all. But that conceivably is also an opportunity. If these voters could be persuaded to show up at the polls in large numbers — much larger than the pollsters are expecting — it could make a big difference, especially in places where there are a lot of them. (JC).

Meanwhile, voters feared for the election process itself, with Democrats worrying about voter suppression and intimidation and Republicans imagining all sorts of voter fraud schemes. One Trump supporter complained to the Sheriff's office in Butler County, Ohio that a voter she saw photographing gravestones must have been engaged in voter fraud. It turned out that the photographer was a registered Republican enjoying, shockingly enough, his favorite hobby.

Then, for one brief moment, the nation could celebrate history together when the Chicago Cubs beat the Cleveland Indians 8-7 in ten innings in one of the wildest, most exciting World Series games ever. The Cubs had last won the Series in another election year, 1908, when the country happily elected Theodore Roosevelt's anointed successor, William Howard Taft. Would it do the same for Barack Obama?

The finish line was now in sight for everyone, and for an exhausted electorate it couldn't come soon enough. With five days to go, there were a few ominous signs for Clinton. For the first time, the Washington Post-ABC News poll showed Trump ahead by a point. It also showed a decline in enthusiasm among Clinton supporters since the issuance of Comey's letter. A lead story in *The Financial*

Times reported: "Wall Street's fear gauge trembles after Clinton poll lead narrows." Gold was up. The Mexican peso was down. The fear gauge, technically something called the Vix index, a measure of expected stock market volatility, was reaching highs not seen since Brexit earlier that year.

The worst news for Clinton may have been the *New York Times*/Siena University Poll giving Trump a four-point lead in Florida. The poll's analyst, Nate Cohn, ascribed Trump's comeback there primarily to a huge swing in support for Trump among Cuban Americans. In September a poll showed that 54% of Cuban Americans supported Obama's stand to end the embargo on Cuba. The poll, however, included recently arrived Cubans not yet eligible to vote. In any event, Trump's support, according to the poll, among Cuban Americans rose from 33% in September to 52% in late October, a change that might have been partially sparked by Obama's order allowing the importation of Cuban rum and cigars and the decision to abstain on the United Nations vote condemning the overall embargo. Many Cubans apparently approved the direction but not the speed with which Obama was moving.

With four days to go, both candidates found themselves in Ohio, with Hillary visiting Cleveland with Beyoncé and Jay Z and Trump staging a rally in Wilmington, Ohio. The day was a study in contrasts. Almost all Clinton's energies now seemed focused on helping get out the vote, particularly among millennials and African-Americans. The two groups formed a large segment of an estimated 10,000 people at the Cleveland rally. Addressing the women, Beyoncé noted, "This is history. There was a time when a woman's opinion did not matter...Look how far we've come from having no voice to being on the brink of history." After the music, Clinton spoke briefly exhorting the audience to remember the lyrics of one of Jay Z's songs: "Rosa Parks sat so Martin Luther could walk and Martin Luther walked so Barack Obama could run and Barack Obama ran so all the children could fly." Then she concluded: "Well, we have more unfinished business to do, more barriers to break, and with your help a glass ceiling to crack once and for all." Meanwhile, Trump, a few hours earlier had been holding a rally in the town of Wilmington, Ohio in which he promised to replace the overworked, aging Brent Spence Bridge in Cincinnati with a new one. How? Trump proposed canceling "billions of dollars in global payments owing to the United Nations." He also suggested fixing Interstate 71 but when this only elicited a tepid crowd reaction, Trump joked, "You're not thrilled by it. Let's not do it, to hell with it." It was estimated that 8000 jobs had been lost in the Wilmington area following the recession of 2008.

The Republican promise of chaos and crisis continued full steam ahead. Rudy Giuliani promised that if Hillary won, "I guarantee in one year she'll be impeached and indicted. It's going to happen. We're going to sort of vote for a Watergate." Republican Senator Richard Burr, fighting to hold on to his seat in North Carolina, raised the specter of Hillary pardoning herself. And Donald Trump simply offered, "Haven't we just been through a lot with the Clintons? The work of government would grind to a halt if she were ever elected." Trump continued to reject the very legitimacy of her candidacy.

As the end of the campaign approached, one thing seemed certain. If volunteer enthusiasm was to decide the election, Trump would win in a landslide, at least if rural and small town Ohio was representative of those areas elsewhere. That was the message implicit in a Cincinnati *Enquirer* headline, "In Ohio, it's Trump energy vs. the Clinton machine, Can enthusiasm beat organization efficiency?" "The story of this election in Ohio," the article began, "can be told by two places: a spot above Ray's Barber Salon in suburban Cincinnati, and a well-lit office in Walnut Hills." Above the barber shop there was a Trump billboard. It turned out it was one of ten scattered through Hamilton County. This was not in itself terribly important until you found out that the ten were financed by volunteers "so enthusiastic they raised the money themselves." In Mahoning County, a key county in northeast Ohio with lots of blue-collar voters, the director of the Trump campaign, who came on board only in September, reported, "People are making their own signs. They're making their own slogans…They come in here. They organize and they go out and flash mob the corners."

Meanwhile, in Clinton's Walnut Hills office, there was a "staging location director" who directed volunteers where they should go with their carefully prepared packets. No one was asking him how to erect billboards. No volunteers were beating down the door. Handcrafted Clinton signs were as plentiful as orchids in the Sahara. The reporters (Jeremy Fugleberg and Deirdre Shesgreen) concluded "…despite a late start and plenty of high-level infighting [within the state G.O.P.], Trump and his Ohio volunteers might yet turn Ohio red, besting the well-organized Clinton campaign behemoth." Trump would, of course, end up winning Ohio by 454,000 votes. Obama won it in 2012 by 166,000. Clinton carried Mahoning County by less than 4,000 votes. Obama had carried it in 2012 by almost 25,000.

If the Clinton campaign had been hoping for a major gaffe by Trump in the last days of the campaign, he was not obliging. In fact, an article in *USA Today* noted, "Donald Trump is pretty much sticking to script in these final days." At the same time he delighted his rallies by constantly reminding himself and his audience of his advisers' instructions: "Stay on point, Donald, stay on point – no sidetracks Donald. Nice and easy, nice." It's just another way that Trump connects with his supporters, as if they're all in on the same secret: that he can't really be himself but it doesn't matter, they love him anyway. The article also reported how Trump's stump speech had developed a recognizable pattern that began with a recitation of the latest favorable polls, then moved to a local issue, such as the drug problem in New Hampshire. He then would move on to his standard attacks on Hillary, Obamacare and the corruption in Washington often leading chants of "Drain the Swamp. " He would conclude by describing all the steps he would take during his first 100 Days as President, his own Contract with America.

On Sunday November 6, the FBI announced that it had concluded its review of the Weiner emails and found nothing to change its decision in July. Trump immediately questioned the FBI's announcement, asserting that it was flat out impossible for the FBI to review 650,000 emails in such a short (9 days) span of time. Of course, he was wrong. Sophisticated software programs apparently were able to identify in relatively short order all the emails on the Weiner device that had been sent from or to Hillary and most turned out to be duplicates of emails previously investigated.

There was no denying, however, how hard Trump was working. On one particularly peripatetic day he actually was able to squeeze in rallies in Iowa, Minnesota, Virginia, Pennsylvania, and Michigan.

One important effect of the Comey letter, as noted, was to change the emphasis of the last week of the Clinton campaign. In *Shattered*, Allen and Parnes report that a clear decision was made to "use more of her cash to throw mud on Trump."

Her end-of-the-race persuasion campaign would be more of a reiteration of the case against Trump. She had to convince voters that he was even worse. 'When the Comey letter hit, we definitely amped up the negative,' said one aide familiar with the change of direction (JA 360).

The campaign's final weekend resembled nothing less than those 1950's roller derby games on black and white television featuring husky, helmeted women trying to crash and elbow their way to victory through equally determined blockers. Trump might have been going down but not without a fight as he crisscrossed the country looking for the one or two states that might push him over the finish line.

Actually, some on Trump's staff, though not apparently Trump himself, were beginning to believe. It would later come out that on the Friday before the election, when a key aide informed Trump that he thought Trump actually had a chance to win, "he looked at me like I was crazy." Brad Parscale might not have been the only one who was thinking this way. Doug Wead reports in his *Game of Thorns* that around this time Bill Clinton got into a shouting match with Hillary on the phone. She was furious at the Comey letter but Bill would have none of it. "Whatever happened to 'It's the economy, stupid' he reportedly shouted. "At the end of the discussion, Bill Clinton took his phone and tossed it off the penthouse roof and watched it sail toward the Arkansas River" (DW 35-36). An aide to Bill Clinton was watching the conversation and said Clinton was so mad, the aide worried he might have a heart attack.

On Monday, November 7, both candidates concluded part of their last day of campaigning with major stops in Pennsylvania, Hillary with a huge nighttime rally on Philadelphia's Independence Mall. She didn't actually come on until 9PM after performances from Bruce Springsteen and Bon Jovi and speeches from both the President and Michelle Obama. Meanwhile, Trump told 5,000 supporters crammed into the gym of Lackawanna College in Scranton, Pennsylvania, "They say we're tied in Pennsylvania. I don't think so. I think we're going to blow them out tomorrow." Earlier in the day, he had spoken in Erie, Pennsylvania and after the Lackawanna speech, he concluded his campaign with stops in Manchester, New Hampshire and then a 1AM rally in Grand Rapids, Michigan.

Then, for the candidates, it was all over.

We still call it Election Day but the term has been becoming less accurate each cycle. As voters went to the polls, the *Associated Press* estimated that at least 43.2 million people had already voted with record levels being reported in 23 states and millions more ballots still coming in. The AP estimated that the ultimate pre-election day figure might be closer to 50 million, roughly 40% of the expected vote.

Despite all the concerns about the process, Election Day itself proved relatively uneventful. As evening came, people began to gather in homes, hotels and campaign headquarters. It wasn't just about the presidency of course. Congressional, gubernatorial and thousands of local races were also to be decided. It was a night one wanted to be with friends.

Most were still expecting a Clinton victory, including myself. I confided to my journal:

> While the final NBC/Wall Street Journal and ABC/Washington tracking polls have Hillary up by four points, the IBD poll (2012's most accurate) actually has her up

by only one. The Des Moines *Register* poll of Iowa voters has her down by seven points, putting that state likely out of reach. Ohio, Florida, and North Carolina seem to be a virtual dead heat. Still, barring any true surprises Hillary should win if she can hold on to Pennsylvania and win either New Mexico or Colorado, meaning she could lose Ohio, New Hampshire, North Carolina and Florida and still gain a majority in the electoral college. There is, of course, another way of looking at this, for if Trump holds his lead in Ohio and wins North Carolina (a Republican state which Romney won in 2012), then he really just needs two states: Florida and Pennsylvania to win the Presidency. In that event, he would have 273 electoral votes even if he loses the other swing states.

That was the entry for November 8. Here is the entry for November 9:

The unthinkable has happened. Donald Trump will be the forty-fifth President of the United States. He ran the table of battleground states he needed just to have a shot – Florida, Ohio and North Carolina – and then broke through the Blue Wall with a vengeance, winning Michigan, Wisconsin and Pennsylvania. He will likely end up north of 300 electoral votes. We had a few friends over to watch the returns. Everyone had left by 11 or so. Except for Pennsylvania, Wisconsin and Michigan, the battleground states pretty much broke as expected. The polls were showing Ohio, Florida and North Carolina in a virtual dead heat or Trump with a modest lead but even if Trump won them all, as he did, he would still have needed another Obama state. The most likely candidates other than Pennsylvania — Nevada and New Hampshire and Colorado — all ended up in Hillary's column. Clearly the Rust Belt states decided the election.

Kellyanne Conway later recalled that as people began calling Trump to congratulate him before Pennsylvania "came in" at 1:36 a.m., Trump kept saying, "Stop congratulating. Stop." Conway attributed this caution, perceptively I think, to the fact that "Mr. Trump is a transactional guy. He's somebody who knows that a deal is not done until it's done."

Then it was done. He had won.

Chapter 2

2016: The Autopsy

The election in 2016 was unique. No presidential election ever featured two more distrusted and disliked major party candidates. Donald Trump scored the lowest of any candidate in the forty-eight year history of the National Election Studies "feeling thermometer" with 38 out of 100 with Hillary right behind him at 41 (MN 16).

By its end, democracy itself seemed somehow tainted. Let me say at the outset that I think Hillary Clinton might have made an excellent President. As a U.S. Senator she had worked well across the proverbial aisle. Even the prickly Senator John McCain admitted he genuinely liked her. Bob Gates, President Obama's Republican Secretary of Defense, admired her and they worked together to increase the influence of their departments vis-à-vis the National Security Council apparatus. That many of her policy proposals might have as well have been written in Sanskrit for all the attention they received was partly the fault of the media but, as will be discussed more fully below, it was hers as well.

My purpose in this Chapter is not to second-guess her strategy nor is it to lament its outcome. We need to understand, however, what the election may have revealed about who we are and how in this highly partisan time we arrived at 2016 at our most important electoral decision in decades.

There has been an enormous amount written about the election that we will attempt to come to grips with in this Chapter. Let me first note a difference in emphasis between how political scientists and most others (chiefly historians and journalists) try to understand political campaigns. Political scientists look at how particular election results fit into long-range patterns of voter behavior and seek to understand the electorate in the context of those patterns. Their focus is on the numbers. They plumb voters' attitudes on issues and feelings about different groups to arrive at a composite portrait of voters and then seek to relate those findings to electoral results themselves. To read today's political science literature without a statistics background (not a personal strongpoint) is like trying to navigate an unfamiliar trail on a moonless night without a flashlight. It can be done but the flashlight sure would help. Political scientists will, of course, consider also the key events in any election, primarily to detect what they call "contingent" happenings to see how they might have affected the final results. The Comey letter late in the campaign is a classic example of one such event.

Historians and journalists, on the other hand, want to grasp the story of the campaign itself. They want to know more about the nitty-gritty details: who had the best organization, the best strategy, the best message, and the best candidate. They want to tell a story. They are, frankly more fun to read but political scientists are indispensable for arriving at some sense of the dynamics of the electorate as a whole. The two angles together offer the best hope of understanding what happened in 2016 and why it happened the way it did.

Not too long ago, it was a truism that the candidate who could best appeal to the center would win because that's where the crucial votes were. Now there is a competing view — the candidate will win who can best mobilize their partisan base — an increasingly ideological base of support because the center, in this view, hardly matters. Indeed, there may not be much of a center to worry about. Polarization is the word used to describe this phenomenon — but what exactly does it mean and who are the polarized? Do the political parties accurately reflect a deeply divided electorate or is there a large center hiding in plain sight that the media and parties no longer care about because it no longer fits their own needs. This is the first question we must confront.

1. How polarized are we?

Polarization, its meaning, extent and causes, is a matter of intense debate among political scientists. Polarization can be thought of in two somewhat different ways. One is ideological divergence. In this meaning, polarization encompasses the world of ideas and opinions. A second meaning refers to the emotional content of our political debates. Can we stand to be in the same room with someone with opposing views without breaking out in a rash? Do we necessarily disrespect those with whom we disagree? If there is one thing that most all scholars in this area agree upon, it is that the elites of the two major parties, specifically those deeply engaged in party politics, including officeholders, are very polarized. As B. Dan Wood (with Soren Jorden) has noted:

> There is virtually no scholarly debate
> over whether party elites in Washington

have polarized. They are. Indeed, the acrimony between Republicans and Democrats in Congress and between Presidents and opposing congressional partisans is so visceral that some observers suggest that Republicans literally hate liberals and Democrats literally hate conservatives (DW 214).

Clearly, Wood's words embrace polarization in both senses and certainly, the larger public sees nothing to contradict this conclusion. The two congressional parties now seem to agree on very little and their disagreements are not only over traditional issues like regulation, taxes and the social safety net but more emotionally charged issues as well: abortion, gun control, and immigration. And, by all accounts, Democrats and Republicans in Congress no longer socialize as they used to and friendships across the aisle are an increasing rarity. The days when Senators Oren Hatch and Ted Kennedy could maintain a genuine friendship and President Ronald Reagan told his staff that we have opponents not enemies seem long gone. It is no accident that the two major pieces of legislation of the last decade – the Affordable Care Act and the Trump tax cuts – were rammed through Congress on party line votes.

As we will see shortly, there seems also to be no question that there is an increasing tendency among at least some in the electorate to view negatively those who disagree with them politically but how deeply these feelings run in the electorate as a whole is not clear. For our purposes, however, the focus in this chapter for the most part is on polarization in the sense of ideological divergence.

There is no question that voting patterns in our general elections are more partisan than ever before. *For the first time in modern history* not a single state in the 2016 election chose a Senator from a different party than the winner of its electoral votes. Events, it should be noted, had been headed in this direction for a long time. As Gary Jacobson has noted, "the vote for House candidates in recent elections is much more tightly linked to the top of the ticket than it was in the 1970's" (GJ 167). In 2012 and 2016 only about one voter in ten cast a split-ticket ballot (GJ 169).

The partisan voting pattern, fortified by regional patterns as well, has had a pronounced effect on presidential campaigns. In 1960, virtually half of the states were fiercely contested with many decided by very small margins. Nixon carried California by 0.5%; Kennedy carried New Jersey by 0.8%; Nixon carried Alaska by 1%; Kennedy carried Missouri by 0.8%; Nixon carried Montana by 2.5%; Kennedy carried New Mexico by 0.8%; Nixon carried Washington by 2.5%; Kennedy carried Texas by 2%, South Carolina by 2.4%, Michigan by 2.1%, and Illinois 0.2%. Kennedy and Nixon actually split the vote nearly evenly in Hawaii with Kennedy ultimately declared the winner by a grand total of 115 votes. In only nine states in 1960 was the winning margin greater than 10%. In 2016, that number rose to thirty-two.

But what has caused this intensely partisan voting pattern? There is no question that today the two major parties divide sharply on a host of issues. We are a long way from 1973 when Justice Lewis Powell could write in one case, "political parties in this country traditionally have been characterized by a fluidity and overlap of philosophy and membership" (Rosario v. Rockefeller 410 U.S. Reports at 769). That statement seems like another epoch in geologic time. Certainly, no one would claim there exist "overlapping philosophies" for the two parties today, except possibly in the broadest sense.

But how did this change take place and what are its implications? Does the undisputed partisan voting pattern reflect an electorate whose views have fundamentally changed? Professor Morris Fiorina of Stanford University questions whether the broad electorate, excluding the most intense partisans, is ideologically divided at all. Other prominent scholars, including Alan Abramowitz and B. Dan Wood, do find an ideologically divided electorate — though there are points of difference between them. Before we go further, let me emphasize that this is a debate that has engaged many academics and it is a subject with many nooks and crannies. My goal in this section is simply to present the discussion in its broadest contours, emphasizing what I think most relevant for understanding our current political situation.

Let me begin with Morris Fiorina. While he agrees that party donors and activists and those on the more extreme ends of the political spectrum have become more much more ideological over the past few decades, he does not believe that this is true of the larger swath of voters. In *Unstable Majorities* he argues (using American National Elections Study or ANES data) that, for the most part, the public's views since 1975 have remained centrist on a variety of issues relating to jobs, government spending, and aid to minorities. Additionally, he points to a Pew Center Research project which had surveyed forty-eight political beliefs and values held by Americans in 1987 and then again in 2012 and found little change. The Pew Report concluded: "The way that the public thinks about poverty, opportunity, business, unions, religion, civic duty, foreign affairs and many other subjects is, to a large extent, the same today as in 1987" (MF 29).

Fiorina also points out how 40% of the electorate (the book was published in 2017) now refuses to identify with either party. This percentage has slowly grown over the past decades.

Many political scientists dismiss this figure on the ground that, when asked, many self-described independents express a preference for one party or the other. Fiorina believes, however, that independents often describe themselves as leaning toward one party or the other at a given time because they have decided to vote for the candidate of that party that year. He shows, relying on a series of studies, that over the course of a four-year period, those "party-leaning" independents do in fact shift allegiances at a frequency much more like true independents than even weak partisans. On this basis, Fiorina asserts that the number of true independents is higher than generally thought. It seems a valid point. Fiorina also points out that only once since 1964 did the winning presidential candidate fail to get a majority of the independent vote. As for 2016, according to the national exit polls, Trump defeated Clinton 46% to 42% among self-described independents (LS 16).

If there are still more true independents than is generally believed and the general public still feels the same about many things as it did in 1987, the picture of a public divided into two armed camps loses some of its force. Reinforcing Fiorina's view is the fact that the national exit polls showed that in 2016 fully 40% of the electorate did not decide for whom to vote until September or later, another indication of a significantly fluid electorate. Indeed, the number of undecided voters very late in the 2016 campaign was much greater than usual. In late October there were three times as many undecided voters as there had been in the 2012 race (JC 108).

So how does Fiorina explain the highly partisan voting patterns where ticket splitting seems a relic of the past? For him, it is a matter of sorting. Specifically, he believes that there is now a constellation of issues that fall in such a way as to encourage the two major parties to maximize the differences between them as a way to promote themselves. In other words, elected representatives benefit from creating the sense that you are on either one team or the other. While acknowledging that the ideologues in both parties are worlds apart, he sees the bulk of voters as still holding relatively moderate views.

Professor Alan Abramowitz sees things differently. He sees little gap between the party elites and the bulk of the party's supporters. Voting patterns, he maintains, reflect deep divisions within society that speak to a real clash of values that have emerged in the nation as a whole over demographic changes and cultural and religious differences. He sees a society increasingly torn between two different visions of reality and aspiration. In his June 2018 book, *The Great Alignment,* he points to such things as the increasingly negative way that voters in each party see the other party. In 1976, for example, only 37% of partisans expressed negative feelings about the other party but by 2012 that figure had grown to 70%. The figure is particularly important because voters with such negative feelings exhibit great party loyalty. In 2012, such voters, according to Abramowitz, voted consistently with their own party 87% of the time as opposed to 68% of partisans with neutral feelings and 52% with positive feelings for the other party (AA 61).

Another key finding for Abramowitz is the way voters of both parties identify themselves. Democrats describing themselves as *very liberal* or *lean liberal* grew from 29% in 1972 to 47% in 2012; Republicans describing themselves as *very conservative* grew from 22% to 51%. Without my getting into a lot of his numbers, Abramowitz also found that while Republicans had become increasingly conservative on virtually the entire spectrum of issues, Democrats remained more moderate on questions involving the role of government in the economy though decidedly more ideological on cultural issues.

The most extensive study of polarization with the deepest historical perspective has been undertaken by Dan Wood and Soren Jordan in *Party Polarization in America: The War Over Two Social Contracts*. Relying on data from the ANES and General Social Survey (GSS), they concluded that "after the 1980s Republicans and Democrats diverged ideologically on specific economic issues, including preferences for the size of government, free markets, taxation, equality of opportunity and the environment." They also found increased ideological divergence on "specific cultural issues, including attitudes on abortion, homosexuality, guns, illegal aliens, and welfare." Significantly, the authors found that much of the increase in ideology on economic issues was attributable to a shift in attitudes among white evangelicals who, since the 1980's, have increasingly adopted traditional conservative positions favoring lower taxes, smaller government, free markets, and less environmental regulation

The Woods/Jordan work analyzes the subject of polarization starting from the very beginning of the republic. Historically, the authors posit two contracts. The initial one was the "Founders' contract," one promoted by the writers of the Constitution, representing the interests of the highly propertied class and favoring low taxes and little regulation. This contract was dominant, in their view, throughout our history until the New Deal that embodied a new contract — one that emphasized the role of the federal government in regulating the marketplace, securing equality of opportunity, and providing a social safety net. For Wood and Jordan, polarization has been a fight between the economically privileged and what they call the "plebian" classes, one that has been with us from the beginning and continues through today. "Party polarization" they write at the outset of their project, "in American history has always been rooted in economic class conflict over who benefits from government and at whose expense" (DW 6). The authors find we are going through a period of strong polarization but they emphasize also that such polarization on economic questions has occurred frequently in our history.

There are other important perspectives on polarization and, for those most interested, I have provided additional discussion in Appendix IV. Our purposes, however, are best served by examining the positions of Professors Fiorina and Abramowitz more critically.

Abramowitz's view of a deeply divided electorate seems on its face at odds with the apolitical character of the American electorate. According to the political scientists Christopher Achen and Larry Bartels in their recent work, *Democracy for Realists*, the one thing voters do not do is carefully consider the policy positions of the candidates in choosing for whom to vote. In fact, the authors' basic view, backed up by a great deal of statistical evidence, is that voters often prefer candidates who don't align well with their stated policy views at all, often then aligning their own positions with the candidate they like rather than the reverse.

Perhaps more damaging for Abramowitz's claim is the simple fact that public opinion surveys on a number of key issues show a majority of Americans in substantial agreement on what might easily be called centrist positions. A comprehensive Pew survey in 2015 showed, for example, 62% of Americans in favor of allowing illegal immigrants to become citizens provided they met certain conditions; another 15% favored allowing them to stay as permanent legal residents though not citizens. Only 19% favored identifying and deporting them. Polls also show that roughly 90% of Americans favor universal background checks and somewhere between 60 and 70% some form of assault weapons ban. Roughly two thirds of the electorate now approves of same-sex marriage and there is even a consensus that abortion should be available in some cases though widespread divergence on how restricted its availability should be.

But if Abramowitz's view confronts some speed bumps, so does Fiorina's. For one thing, it does not seem to account for the great growth in the negative way Democrats and Republicans view each other or the growing numbers of parents who express dismay at the idea that their child would bring home a supporter of the other party. Shanto Lyengar, a Stanford political scientist, believes that the public is very much polarized in terms of how it views others holding different views, believing that voters have come to see agreement as a "litmus test" for character and arguing that "we have good evidence that inter-personal relationships are increasingly constrained by party politics" (SL).

Fiorina's view also seems at odds with the decline in ticket splitting. In 1981, 24 states had split representation in the U.S. Senate, with one Republican and one Democrat. In the newly elected Congress beginning January 2019, the number is 9, including the one state represented by a Republican and Independent. Why should this be the case if the country as a whole is still basically centrist? Something is happening here even if we don't understand it completely.

Abramowitz's view of a deeply divided public also feels right when one considers the extent to which voters now trust entirely different messengers. An *Economist/YouGov* poll taken between October 16 and 18, 2016 revealed that 79% of Clinton supporters deemed *The New York Times* trustworthy or very trustworthy while 70% of Trump supporters thought the paper untrustworthy or very untrustworthy. The divide was even more striking with cable news. Only 10% of Trump supporters saw CNN as trustworthy/very trustworthy as compared to 69% of Clinton supporters. The cleavages were as dramatic for other news sources, Clinton supporters trusting the Huffington Post and MSNBC, Trump supporters hardly at all, the reverse being true for Fox News and Breitbart, though almost half of Trump supporters refused to characterize Breitbart as either trustworthy or untrustworthy.

One other point seems somehow to better fit with Abramowitz's view. David Wasserman of the Cook Political Report has calculated that "the share of voters living in extreme landslide counties, quintupled from 4% to 21%" between 1992 and 2016. This suggests — though I admit that this is pure speculation — that the extreme partisan divide has been helped along by the way in which neighbors and friends reinforce each other's biases, perhaps as those on the more ideological end of the spectrum talk to their less politically minded neighbors.

Is the Fiorina view of a centrist electorate incompatible with the Abramowitz view of a more ideological one? Perhaps not, particularly if one posits a distinctly layered electorate, the top layer being the roughly one-fifth who are deeply engaged in politics, the other four-fifths more or less disengaged except at election time when they become an important part of the drama. For a brief period, the parties and candidates encourage this latter group to not only vote but to feel as if the whole world depends on how they vote. Given the present state of our politics, a generally disengaged electorate is suddenly made to feel that there is a *take no prisoners* partisan war at stake whose outcome depends on the complete domination of one side over the other. That is certainly the impression that the elites of both parties try to create and certainly the Trump presidency has done nothing to attenuate.

But why have the parties and candidates been so successful in carving us up into such clearly defined voting blocs? I think it has a great deal to do with recent history and the high degree of emotionalism that a number of issues arouse. Let me elaborate further.

Prior to 2000, though there was certainly much partisanship, it is also true that most of the key legislation enacted in the last two decades of the twentieth century attracted the votes of both Democrats and Republicans. This included a landmark piece of bipartisan tax reform legislation during the Reagan years, the Americans With Disabilities Act, and a major civil rights bill during the George H.W. Bush years, as well as the approval of NAFTA and a major revision to the federal welfare system under Clinton.

A measure of the distance between then and now can be seen in Newt Gingrich's Contract with America. It seems almost quaint compared to the issues of today. The following are the pieces of legislation which Gingrich promised to bring to the floor within the first 100 days of a Republican controlled Congress: a proposal for a balanced budget amendment to the Constitution; an anti-crime package; an act to discourage illegitimacy and teen pregnancy; a bill to strengthen child support enforcement; a $500 per child tax credit; a prohibition of U.S. troops being placed under United Nations command; a bill to raise the social security earnings limit; small business incentives; a "loser pays" bill to discourage frivolous litigation; and a first ever vote on term limits for Congress.

Not a word in the Contract about guns, immigration, deregulation, tax cuts, health care, income inequality, the environment, energy, global warming, religious freedom, globalization, or drugs.

Then came the twenty-first century and with it 9/11; the Iraq War; the greatest economic crisis since the Great

Depression; the emergence of climate change as a global issue; the debilitating effect of the constant threat of terrorism; the transition to an economy that has widened both the economic and social gap between the more and less educated; the explosion in the deficit; mass murders in schools, nightclubs, churches, synagogues and public plazas; the accumulation of a trillion dollar debt load by the nation's students; the rise of the internet and accompanying phenomena such as hacking, cyber bullying and fake news; the grotesque mushrooming of mass incarceration (we now imprison a higher proportion of our citizens than any nation on earth, including Russia and Cuba); the growing controversy over how to treat the nation's millions of undocumented workers and secure our southern border; and a drug crisis of unprecedented proportions which kills more people in a year than soldiers who died during the entire Vietnam War.

Add to all of this that the real wages of high school educated men have fallen 40% since 1970 (AH 125) and you have some inkling of the depth of anger in what many fear is a vanishing middle class.

For former factory workers, there is something else. Fifty years ago roughly 55% of the workforce was engaged in manufacturing. Today that figure is 10%. When factories disappear, so does a way of life. The loss of a way of life involves not just forgoing a good paycheck but a sense of producing something and living in a community that knows what it is about. Employers who move jobs overseas are breaking a bond or perhaps revealing that one never existed in the first place. I wonder whether the depth of the anger that Trump tapped into, particularly among middle-aged non-college educated white men, can be explained not only by the disappearance of a job or a paycheck but the loss of everything familiar, a feeling of falling into the rabbit hole. It is one thing to face reversals in a setting that one still recognizes; it is quite another to sense one's world completely disappearing.

The relative decline of the working class can be traced in other ways as well, perhaps best encapsulated in one statistic: in 1980, labor's share of the national income was 73%; in 2005, it was 64% (PS 136) and it is not likely to have improved much since then. As Paul Starr has observed, "In recent decades, as part-time, temporary, and other forms of precarious work have increased, the people who do those jobs have often not received the benefits and protections accorded standard employment" (PS 139).

So there are good reasons for the emotionalism that now pervades our political discourse. For many liberals, the very survival of the planet is at stake with global warming. For gun owners, the right of self-defense requires constant vigilance with no quarter given. Members of the LGBT community rightly worry about keeping their hard won gains. Many on the religious right regard freedom of conscience as under constant assault from an increasingly hostile secular world. African-Americans simply want to be able to go about their business free of police harassment and worse. The long-term unemployed and underemployed yearn simply for a decent job, health care, and the ability to raise their family. For millions of women, the fight is for the right to control their own bodies and work in a non-sexist environment.

Politics is no longer a game for the elites because the issues cut right to the bone for tens of millions of Americans. In the fifties, sixties and seventies, those who said that they cared a good deal about who won the presidential election fluctuated in the 60% range. Since the year 2000, it has fluctuated in the 80% range (MF 23). The politically disengaged portion of the electorate may not follow issues closely or think about them much, but they do have instincts that are easily exploited by politicians wishing to exaggerate differences and make every disagreement a matter of life and death. And demonizing the other side is a handy way of avoiding talking about issues per se. In a different political atmosphere, the many areas in which voters agree could become a much more important part of the political equation.

Defining the two layered electorate a little more sharply: the first is composed of those who care so deeply or are so politically engaged that they set the terms of the political debate and often have an outsized impact on the nominating process of their respective parties and the second is a largely centrist, somewhat disengaged (though less so than in prior years) electorate that is not itself organized well enough to change the toxic political ditch we have landed in but who will still often determine the outcome of closely contested general elections.

Whatever the cause of the partisan pattern of voting, the fact that 2016 turned out as well as it did for Trump should not be surprising once we see how well Republicans in general fared. Indeed, it might be said that the increasingly partisan voting patterns of the last two decades laid the real foundation for Trump's victory to which Trump added his own unique appeal to a group of voters not previously energized by either party.

Let's now turn to the election itself, examining in Section 2 below, the nature of Trump's appeal to voters and in Section 3 the actual events of the campaign. Section 2 focuses mainly on voter attitudes, Section 3 on the candidates and their campaigns.

2. Examining Trump's appeal

Not long after Trump's victory, a debate broke out among Clinton supporters whether economic or racial anxiety was the most important factor in explaining the election result. In April 2017, Bernie Sanders at a rally in Boston noted, "Some people think that the people who voted for Trump are racists and sexists and homophobes and deplorable folks." Sanders disagreed, asserting instead that Trump supporters voted for him because of their "fierce opposition to an economic and political system that puts wealthy and corporate interests over their own." Elizabeth Warren, attending the same rally, concurred.

Of course, racial anxiety and feelings of economic vulnerability can feed on each other so to some extent this may be a false dichotomy. In any event, I argue in subsection (b) below that explaining Trump's support is not a simple matter and that no one single aspect of the electorate can fully account for it. I also question a number of studies focusing on racial anxiety in particular.

I begin, however in subsection (a) with a brief discussion of Trump's campaign rallies. It has been estimated that only 12% of his supporters attended those rallies or knew someone who did. Thus, to base one's image of the typical Trump voter on what was sometimes very unacceptable behavior at these events — and those guilty did not constitute the majority at those events, many coming as families — is obviously stereotyping on steroids.

After discussing the competing explanations given for Trump's success, I try and let his supporters speak for themselves, focusing in subsections (c) and (d) on voters in the Rust Belt States that decided the election.

a. *The rallies*

Trump's rise was not entirely unpredictable, for into this troubled and uncertain world stepped a charismatic celebrity of significant personal wealth already known to tens of millions of Americans as a television personality, a candidate who, unlike virtually all the others, could not possibly be held complicit in the politics that many voters had come to abhor. For those voters, the Trump rogue personality and projection of enormous self-confidence were reasons to vote for him.

The simple fact is that even a year before the election Trump was drawing tremendous crowds, including 20,000 in Mobile, Alabama, 4,000 in Phoenix, Arizona, and 10,000 in Springfield, Illinois where, Katy Tur reports, Trump truthfully claimed that he had beaten out Elton John's crowd at the same venue and without a piano. She adds: "Trump supporters wait in lines that wrap around blocks. They say *The Art of the Deal* changed their lives. They ask Trump to sign dollar bills" (KT 51).

What could account for this extraordinary outpouring? Certainly Trump's celebrity status was important but Jennie Johnson of the Washington Post also put her finger on something important when she noted in early January 2016 how so many of the towns Trump visited were lagging behind their home state on a number of measures including median income, rates of home ownership, and number of residents with college degrees (JJ). At these rallies, Johnson observes, Trump "presents himself as an underdog of sorts who beat the system with some basic common sense and his biggest cheers often come when he bashes Democrats, the Republican establishment, the media, money-grubbing corporations and any other institution that let people down."

The rallies did of course have their darker side. In his book, *The People Are Going to Rise Like the Waters Upon Your Shore,* Jared Sexton describes how he became an overnight social media sensation and soon the object of harassment and death threats when he provided his eyewitness account of a Trump rally in Greensboro, North Carolina. It remains disturbing reading even today: "The media was penned into an area by railings and the reporters made notes on legal pads or tapped out their reports on laptops while, a few feet away, supporters in the scrum by the stage were busy venting their anger and spewing racist and misogynistic slurs" (JS 198). Bumper stickers like "If only Hillary had married OJ instead" were not uncommon sights at Trump rallies (JS 5).

In her memoir of the campaign, *Unbelievable*, Tur remembers one time when the candidate mused about the possibility of killing the press, finally dismissing it but making it seem, in a joking way, as if it was a close call. Tur and NBC became a special focus of Trump's attention actually forcing NBC to provide private security for Tur outside all his rallies. Protesters did infiltrate Trump's rallies leading to the occasional sucker punch and though Trump never "explicitly condoned the violence at his rallies, he never condemned it either" even musing at one event how he would like to punch one particular protestor in the mouth (KT 176). At another rally he shouted that that he would pay the legal bills of a white audience member who had punched a Black protestor who was already in the process of being evicted. On another occasion, he shouted how he'd like to punch a protestor in the face.

As disturbing as the tone and some incidents at his rallies were to others, Trump could make them exciting and even fun. At a mid-October rally in Newtown Township in Bucks County, Pennsylvania, Trump spotted two-year-old Hunter Tirpak. Trump realized that he had seen Hunter a week and a half earlier at the Mohegan Sun Arena in Wilkes-Barre, Pa. Tirpak's mother had dressed him in a dark suit, white shirt and red tie, just like the Donald. Now here he was again. Bring him up here, the candidate implored his mother and she did. Cradled in Trump's arms, Trump asked Hunter, "Do you want to go back to mommy or stay with Donald Trump?" "Trump" the boy replied as the arena erupted in cheers. Corey Lewandowski described even early pre-nomination Trump rallies in these terms: "Our events were like rock concerts. He came out to 'Rockin in the Free World' and it was something that people were energized about (Institute 44)."

Trump's rallies were extraordinarily helpful to him for a number of reasons. They energized him. They were almost always accompanied by extensive interviews with local media, an important point for a campaign that wished to bypass national media thought to be hostile. And perhaps most importantly, they allowed supporters to see just how many of each other there were. Benjamin Bradlee Jr. in *The Forgotten*, for example, describes how a huge rally outside Wilkes-Barre the day before the Pennsylvania primary was "a revelation of sorts for many local residents – some of whom had been embarrassed to express their public support for the turbulent and contentious candidate" (BB 14).

As helpful as his rallies may have been for Trump, we need to look elsewhere to understand his appeal. Why were all those people there in the first place and why so crazed for him?

b. *The Debate over Trump's Appeal*

I noted above the intense debate between those on the one hand who look to racial resentment and fear of diversity as the key explanations for Trump's success and those on the other hand who point to economic fears and anxiety.

E.J. Dionne Jr., Thomas E. Mann, and Norman J. Ornstein (the "co-authors") of *One Nation After Trump* attempt to reconcile the two viewpoints by first agreeing that there is strong evidence to support the race and cultural perspective, but adding:

But if race and culture mattered a great deal in 2016, there is significant evidence that swing voters who went for Trump (as against solid Republicans and voters who constituted his base in the GOP primaries) may have been more motivated by economics than other parts of his constituency (ED 166).

This is a useful distinction though given Jenna Johnson's observations above, I'm not sure I would agree that Trump's primary base was not also motivated in large part by economic considerations. Nevertheless, there is no denying the fact that the Republican Party as a whole has become the natural home for those who seek to limit legal immigration, favor the most draconian efforts to curb illegal immigration, and worry about the effects of an increasingly diverse population. It seems to me that the studies emphasizing the importance of race and culture are really describing what Trump's Republican Party has become but do not present a compelling case for what caused voters to switch from Obama to Trump or why he was able to bring out so many voters who had never voted before or hadn't voted in a long time. In emphasizing the economic concerns of swing voters, the co-authors cited one study showing how Trump did better than Romney in more than half of the country's metropolitan areas, including Buffalo, Providence, Detroit, Cleveland, and St. Louis, all of which had suffered from severe deindustrialization. Another study found that the slower a county's job growth since 2007, the greater the shift toward Trump (ED 167). Still a third cited study concluded that Trump beat Clinton in counties where jobs were more at risk because of technology and globalization.

I could end my brief examination of this debate here because I've already indicated my belief that the co-authors are quite right in distinguishing between swing voters and solid Republicans.

However, with a little trepidation, I do want to flesh out my reasons for believing that the claims of racial resentment may themselves be overstated.

These studies include one by three political scientists from the University of Massachusetts. "the U of M Study," (BS) that concluded that by far the most important predictor of Trump support was the degree to which non-college educated Trump voters tended to deny that racism remained a significant problem in the country. Another study conducted by Diana Mutz of the University of Pennsylvania (the Mutz study) concluded that support for Trump was related to "the changes in the [Democratic] party's positions on issues related to American global dominance and the rise of majority-minority issues that threaten white Americans' sense of dominant group status." A third examination by Professor Abramowitz in *The Great Alignment* echoed the findings of these two studies concluding, "The difference between white voters with and without college degrees in support for Trump is almost entirely explained by racial/ethnic resentment (AA 159)." Abramowitz argues that this phenomenon was no accident citing how "stoking racial fear and resentment was a central element of Trump's strategy" (AA 124). Finally there is the work of Sean McElwee and Jason McDaniel appearing in the Nation (the "McElwee Study") emphasizing fear of racial diversity as a key to understanding the Trump voter.

Let me start with Abramowitz's conclusion on racial resentment of African-Americans. Obviously, it rests in the first place on the validity of his approach to assessing racial resentment. That assessment was based on the voters' responses to whether they agreed or disagreed with the following assertions:

(1) Irish, Italian, Jewish, and many other minorities overcame prejudice and worked their way up. Blacks should do the same without any special favors.

(2) Generations of slavery and discrimination have created conditions that make it difficult for Blacks to work their way out of the lower class.

(3) Over the past few years, Blacks have gotten less than they deserve.

(4) It is really a matter of some people not trying hard enough; if Blacks would only try harder they could be just as well off as whites.

Do these questions really measure resentment with the kind of animus resentment usually implies? Not necessarily.

While Statement (1) does suggest a negative attitude toward affirmative action programs, "special favors" is itself such a pejorative term that anyone might agree with it without necessarily being resentful toward Blacks. Indeed, 46% of white Obama voters in 2012 actually agreed with this statement (JS 162). Statement No. 2 asks the voter to link the historical condition of slavery and discrimination with the current problems of the Black lower class, but clearly a negative answer could simply reflect a belief that those historical conditions are no longer holding Blacks back today. In an era of affirmative action and a Black president, such an answer is hardly grounds for inferring racial resentment or anxiety. Disagreement with the third statement might simply reflect a belief that Blacks have gotten no more or less than what they deserve, hardly the basis for finding racial resentment. Again, a voter survey of 2012 showed 49% of white Obama voters disagreeing with this statement. The fourth statement does express a negative attitude toward Blacks as a group but it seems an unlikely explanation for voter resentment, much less motivation, since it assumes that whites are in fact doing better than Blacks.

I would suggest that the same infirmity that affects Abramowitz's conclusions also affect the Mutz and U. of Mass. studies. Mutz discovers racial anxiety, for example, in the agreement of Trump voters with the statement "the American way of life is threatened," asserting that this is an adequate basis for concluding that Trump supporters feared the loss of white dominance. Such an equivalence assumes that Trump supporters equated the American way of life primarily with white dominance and that this was a significant factor in deciding for whom to vote. I would argue, however, that voters could be thinking of any number of things in lamenting the loss of the American way of life, including growing secularization, loss of manufacturing jobs, a feeling of disrespect for traditional values, and all the changing mores that have come with the Internet and social media. A similar infirmity affects the U. of Mass. study. Believing that racism is no longer a problem in this country does not shed much light on why voters decided to choose Donald Trump.

The McElwee study concluded that "our analysis indicates that Donald Trump successfully leveraged existing resentment towards African-Americans in combination with existing fears of increasing racial diversity in America to reshape the presidential electorate, strongly attracting nativists towards Trump and pushing some more affluent and highly educated people with more cosmopolitan views to support Hillary Clinton" (SM). These conclusions were also based on the answers to four questions, this time about how rising diversity would impact the nation. Voters were advised that census projections show that by 2043 racial minorities would constitute a majority of the nation and then were asked, "Thinking about the likely impact of this coming demographic change, how much [do] you agree with each of these statements:

    1. Americans will learn more from one another and be enriched by exposure to many different cultures.
    2. A bigger, more diverse workforce will lead to more economic growth.
    3. There will be too many demands on government services.
    4. There will not be enough jobs for everybody.

The study concluded that "probability of support for Trump increases sharply with negative views on diversity." If the key debate is between those emphasizing racial and cultural factors and those emphasizing economic factors in Trump's victory, I am not sure how much this study helps clarify the issue given particularly how the second and fourth statements also clearly measure voters fears for their economic future. Also, I wonder how much an examination asking voters to predict the future impact of a development not expected for another quarter century can fully explain voter motivation in 2016.

I do not mean that these analyses are not of value. All four studies add to our profile of the electorate but I'm not sure they advance our understanding as to why Trump won. In 2016, more than 200 counties having less than 50,000 voters switched from supporting President Obama, sometimes by wide margins, to supporting President Trump, sometimes by equally wide margins. There is simply no direct evidence that racial attitudes had changed so markedly in these counties as to account for this shift in support, nor do these studies offer any evidence that race was a conscious factor in how voters made up their mind. Was there any focus at all during the Obama administration on the problems of rural America? Did the Obama years give rural and exurban America any reason to want to keep the presidency in Democratic hands? Did the Obama administration show any special concern for the plight of the displaced factory worker in the rust belt states? Couldn't these have been important factors in Trump's success?

And another reason why all the emphasis on race may be misplaced: *Trump only bettered Mitt Romney's totals among white voters by one percentage point. Romney won the white vote by twenty percentage points (fifty-nine to thirty-nine), Trump by twenty-one (fifty-eight to thirty-seven).*

Even in *Identity Crisis* by John Sides, Michael Tesler, and Lynn Vavreck, a well researched and thoughtful examination of the 2016 election, the authors provide no direct evidence of changes in racial attitudes that might account for Trump's conversion of so many Obama supporters to his side. Rather they argue, "The election turned on the group identities that the candidates had activated — and these identities help explain why Trump won the electoral college" (JS 9).

The authors' key finding was that "growing alignment of group identities and partisanship is crucial because it gives these group identities more political relevance" (JS 4). While the authors place great salience in racial identity, they do not believe that anger and anxiety were much different than they had been in previous elections: "…levels of anger and anxiety were no greater in 2016 than in recent years. In fact, economic anxiety had been *decreasing* not increasing in recent years" (JS 7). The authors conclude that "the landscape implied both a toss-up election and one that was ripe for racially charged divisiveness" (JS 7). I would briefly note that the studies cited by E.J. Dionne and company do suggest that economic anxiety had not been decreasing as asserted in *Identity Crisis*. The Sides book does show how strongly the Republican and Democratic parties now divide along racial and ethnic lines but that has been the case for many years with its origins going all the way back to the passage of the Civil Rights Acts in the mid-nineteen sixties.

I should note that in her memoir, Hillary Clinton does embrace the racial identity perspective. She cites an exit poll finding that Trump voters' top concerns were immigration and terrorism — a finding that incidentally is not supported by other evidence. Clinton concludes "That's a polite way of saying many of those voters were worried about people of color – especially Blacks, Mexicans, and Muslims — threatening their way of life" (HC 413). I find this an extraordinary statement. Is fear of terrorism really inextricably bound up with deep racial bias and, for that matter, does a fear about the economic consequences of immigration for one's future also point in that same direction? I think not.

I do not mean to minimize the degree of racial animus in the country as a whole. A recent book by Jonathan Metzl, *Dying of Whiteness*, provides ample evidence as to how deeply racial stereotypes can run, how white voters, for example, receiving huge benefits from Medicaid can rail against Medicaid expansion. But the fact is that deciding for whom to vote for President is an enormously complicated process that voters often struggle with. It is the reason, particularly in 2016 when both candidates were viewed so negatively, that there were so many undecided voters so late in the campaign. Frankly, to better understand what happened it is important to simply listen to what voters said.

In *The Great Revolt*, Saleno Zito and Brad Todd (a journalist and a Republican pollster) did just that, seeking out Trump voters in four Rust Belt states (Pennsylvania, Ohio, Michigan, and Wisconsin) and Iowa. What emerges is a complex picture that should remind everyone of the enormous range of factors that go into deciding how one will vote for President. Here is a representative sample.

Dave Rubbico from Erie County Pennsylvania, a blue collar Democrat if there ever was one, voted for Obama twice but was deeply disappointed with Obama's second term and the way he "pussyfooted" around problems: "He was too much with delicate diplomacy and not enough for action." For him, the contrast with Trump was stark and in Trump's favor:

> Look this isn't complicated, in fact it is pretty simple. I wanted Barack Obama to succeed. He ended up hurting us. He was weak, Donald Trump? Well, we finally have someone who has the balls to say what needs to be said and then goes out and does what he says (SZ 48).

Connie Knox from Lee County, Iowa had also voted for Obama: "I foolishly campaigned for him because I thought Martin Luther King would have loved to see this day when a Black man could be President." She described herself as in agreement with Republicans on fiscal responsibility, small government, and "most definitely the Second Amendment." She also agreed, however, with Democrats "on things like making sure the people who can't take care of themselves are taken care of. I also have a problem that the Republicans can't take their nose out of people's bedrooms." In the end, she was drawn to Trump's independent streak. She had also read *The Art of the Deal* and decided Trump was much smarter than people gave him credit for (SZ 53-59).

Seventy-year old Rose Zuba from Luzerne County Pennsylvania grew up very poor, has been "going with" the same gentleman for forty-six years and had never voted in a presidential election until 2016. "For as long as I can remember, I thought of professional politicians as *the* problem," she said, but Trump registered as someone different. "Going out there to vote for him really meant something to me. I don't know how to explain it except I felt compelled not for me, but for my country (SZ 64)."

Lake County, Michigan is the poorest in the state of Michigan. It went from giving Barack Obama a 12 point margin in 2008 to giving Trump a 23 point margin in 2016. Cindy Hutchins was one of those who switched. Her change seemed partly due to concrete things like her health insurance premiums going up 50% (something she blamed on Obamacare) and her belief that fiscally the country was out of control. But there was also something deeper, a feeling that the Democratic Party was no longer the voice of the people, as they had been in the Democratic union household where she grew up:

> You know one of the things I don't get about the Democratic Party or the news media is the lack of respect they give to people who work hard all of their lives to get themselves out of the hole. It is as though they want to punish us for the very things we hold dear: hard work, no dependence on the government, no debt, and so on.

For Renee Diubble, a resident of Ashtabula County, Ohio — which President Obama carried in 2012 by 13 points and Trump by 19 in 2016 — the attraction to Trump was "instant:"

> What Trump had to say was as if he had been part of my community all of my life; he understood the economic problems, the decay of our society, and that drain of our treasure, our children, out of our communities because there are no jobs, or future in Ashtabula County.

The Trump rally in Geneva, Ohio marked the first time a presidential candidate had come to the Ashtabula County since John Kennedy in 1960. Renee didn't find the rally negative at all. In fact, "to me it was really exciting. We had our banners — we still have them. The Trump banners. I like got one in every color." She adds: "It's not that I think he is perfect, but we didn't want perfect. The reason, I think, and my husband will tell you the same darn thing too, it's because he tells it like it is…that's why we would get along real well, him and I."

Christine Borglin and Amy Giles-Maurer from Kenosha County, Wisconsin represented a whole subset of feminists who the authors discovered were deeply worried about preserving their Second Amendment rights. The NRA spent a reported $35 million to convince these voters that their right to defend their homes and their children would be as good as gone if Clinton were elected. The Clinton campaign never offered a significant rebuttal.

This was one group that didn't need to like Trump in order to vote for him. "I'll tell you," said Christine Borglin, "I did not feel good about voting for Trump at all. Because I didn't like him. I just didn't like him. But I knew things that were important to me were at stake, like the direction of the Supreme Court and the protection of gun rights."

The fact that Borglin admitted to intensely disliking Hillary Clinton, citing the email scandal, probably made her decision much easier.

The Supreme Court was also a critical factor among the many Christian women for whom the thrice-married Trump was not a natural choice. Julie Bayles admitted that she voted for Trump reluctantly but was convinced that "he was going to be a warrior for people of faith. He wasn't going to let us down, and that would begin with his Supreme Court choices."

These brief descriptions easily attest to the wide range of reasons people had for voting for Trump. One common theme was how much these voters felt neglected by the professional politicians in both parties. In the Appendix of *The Great Revolt*, the authors reported on a survey of 2,000 self-reporting Trump supporters (400 from each of the Rust Belt states and Iowa). Remarkably, 89% of those surveyed agreed with the statement, "Republicans and Democrats in Washington are both guilty of leading the country down the wrong track."

One can't read *The Great Revolt* without a strong feeling that Trump's outsider status, his wealth, his being a television celebrity, his ability to connect with his audience, and his reputation as "a tough son of a bitch" in the words of Bobby Knight were enormous advantages for him. On the other hand, liberal anger (myself included) over Trump's demonizing of illegal immigrants might have led many of us to exaggerate the importance of these attacks for Trump voters, believing that what mattered a great deal to us must have also mattered a great deal to Trump voters as well. That, at least, is a reasonable conclusion to draw from another response in the Appendix survey. It specified four of Trump's campaign promises and asked his supporters to rank them in order of importance, 34% ranked bringing back manufacturing jobs to

America as most important; 30% protecting Medicare and Social Security; 28% putting conservatives on the U.S. Supreme Court; and only 7% building a wall on our border with Mexico (SZ 23).

Given the concern about the Supreme Court, Trump's listing of the conservative judges from whom he would pick his Supreme Court nominee was a strategic masterstroke. It was mentioned numerous times by voters interviewed for *The Great Revolt*. Said one voter: "What really changed it for me was when he came out with that list of Supreme Court nominees. Then it was all over, all over — I was in" (SZ 200).

d. *Luzerne County, Pennsylvania*

No county in the United States has been more thoroughly dissected in trying to understand how Donald Trump became President than Luzerne County, Pennsylvania. It has been the subject of numerous journalistic explorations and then, in October 2018, the subject of an important book by Ben Bradlee Jr. entitled "The Forgotten." Located in the northeast part of the State, about equidistant from New York City and Philadelphia, it is a county of roughly 310,000 people with a far from unique history, one marked initially by post-war prosperity when coal mining and manufacturing were king and then by a sharp decline as the mines petered out and globalization took thousands of manufacturing jobs away. At present, more than one in five Luzerne County families with children live in poverty with per capita income slightly under $25,000, which is $4,500 below the state average (BB 38).

Prior to 2016, Luzerne County had voted Democratic in presidential elections for 20 years. President Barack Obama carried the County by ten percentage points in 2008 and by more than five percentage points in 2012.

Trump carried the County by 20 percentage points, a total swing of 30 points since 2008. Maybe the result should not have been a surprise; Trump won 77% of the county's vote in the Republican primary against the remaining candidates Ted Cruz and John Kasich (BB 13) and in 2016 more than 5000 voters had switched their affiliation from Democratic to Republican in order to vote in the Republican primary.

Still, Trump's success in the county was a radical departure for a county where most local officials are Democrats, and party affiliation, in the words of Jim Kunhenn, who spent two months after the election in Luzerne County preparing an article for the Washington *Monthly*, is "passed on as a birthright." Kunhenn, like Bradlee Jr., conducted in depth interviews with many Trump supporters. His conclusion is an important one for those looking to 2020:

> What happened in Luzerne County in 2016 is as much a part of a national story—echoing trends that occurred around the country—as it is an intensely local story, marked by values and history. As Democratic leaders seek to rally the party around a new, distinct economic message, the story of Luzerne underscores the challenges they face. (JK)

Kunhenn found that Luzerne County was not without assets. "Its location is ideal for outdoor recreation; it's a transportation intersection located two hours from the major metro areas of New York and Philadelphia. It has a solid health care infrastructure, with two major hospital systems and a concentration of quality higher education institutions."

Even as late as the 1990s, the County enjoyed some important manufacturing. But then in 2001 it lost a television production plant that relocated to Mexicali, Mexico; in 2004 an important cathode ray tube plant closed its doors. Area residents blamed NAFTA for both closures. Then came the financial crisis of 2008 from which the recovery has been slow and much less robust than in other parts of the state. Sue Henry, a talk radio host on WILK-FM, recalled for Kuhnhenn the voices of despair that had been calling in for nine years and asked him to "imagine men at the peak of their earning potential, their wages suddenly flat-lined or reversed. They had to dip into their 401Ks just to buy groceries. Nine years later, they are still suffering an economic hangover."

With manufacturing jobs gone, residents work in warehouses and the healthcare system for a fraction of the pay they formerly received. There seems very little future for a young person. It was why a single mom was so happy when her son got his electrician's license since it meant he was free to leave the area. Kuhnhenn reports that a 2016 survey in 10 local colleges and universities found only one-third of students willing to stay in the area even if they could find jobs.

I will discuss more in Chapter 4 how I think Democrats can win some of these voters back but it begins with understanding that in 2008, men and women of Luzerne County voted for Obama not to make racial history but because he represented "change you can believe in" and because he talked strongly about taking on the special interests. That change, in Luzerne County's eyes, never happened and then the Democrats selected in 2016 a candidate even more closely identified with the very Wall Street crowd that they believed caused their misery. As John Yudichak, the Democratic State Senator who represents Luzerne County, told Ben Bradlee Jr., "Obama had hope and change, Trump had knock-down-the-door and change."

In early October 2016, Hazleton, Luzerne's largest town with roughly 25,000 people, was the subject of a major *New York Times* article. In it, Republican Congressman Lou Barletta, formerly Mayor of Hazelton, predicted that Trump is "going to win here and win big." The article adds another dimension to understanding the forces at work in Luzerne County.

Hazelton's Hispanic population grew from 4.9% in 2000 to 37% in 2010 and 46% in 2014. Barletta was quoted as attributing much of Trump's support in the region to the resentments, both cultural and economic, created by this influx among white voters. Barletta himself was fully in tune with Trump's stance having actually led the successful fight for the first ordinance in the nation (subsequently nullified by the courts) that would have penalized employers and landlords who engaged with illegal immigrants.

Barletta's prediction proved accurate because he knew intimately the concerns of his own voters. Nick Zapotocky voted for Obama in 2008 and owned a motorcycle shop in Hazelton, but blamed illegal immigration for the rise in crime in Hazelton. Another voter, a 70-year-old retiree, had recently moved out of Hazelton because he no longer felt safe. There was also economic resentment. Wana Bostic, a home health care worker who made $11.50 an hour, felt that her wages would be higher but for the depressing effect on wages of available Hispanic labor. Everyday cultural clashes had also spread resentment among whites, including some who said that Hispanics play their music too loud at night, make no effort to learn English, and fail to observe ordinary driving and pedestrian rules.

These were certainly the voters for whom Trump's anti-immigration message clearly resonated, but they were not the full story, for Hazelton was making a comeback, sparked by the creation of a tax-free economic development zone that had attracted businesses ranging from a Cargill meat packing plant to an Amazon warehouse. Hispanics make up a large portion of the workforce. They too would have something to say about the election, for more than 800 new Hispanic voters had been registered in Hazelton, expanding voting rolls in Hazelton by 10%. Interestingly, the article also reported on some lifelong Republicans who planned to vote for Clinton, like Stephen Schleicher, a dermatologist, one-third of whose patients were now Hispanic and who felt that the city would have been "a white ghost town" but for the "revitalization" of the city.

In the end, however, Luzerne County gave Trump a stunning victory. Ben Bradlee Jr. has offered what for me is a nuanced and convincing explanation for what happened in Lucerne County:

> By the time of the 2016 presidential campaign, a postindustrial malaise had settled over Luzerne, along with a growing anger and frustration over the tectonic cultural, demographic and economic shifts that the white working class, at least, seemed ready to assign bipartisan blame to. It was the perfect moment for a non-ideological and malleable populist to emerge, a candidate nominally a Republican but who didn't seem wedded to either party: Donald J. Trump (BB 39).

The remarkable thing was how perfectly Trump with his simple language and willingness to be politically incorrect captured Luzerne voter's imagination. This is what struck Sue Henry when she told Ben Bradlee Jr:

The affinity people had here for Trump was amazing. My listeners said: he's our guy. Yes, I said but he's been married three times. They didn't care. They never wavered People were so loyal. They would never give up... They believed they had been left behind, mostly economically (BB 40).

Could Clinton have done anything about this state of affairs? Could she somehow have better blunted the effectiveness of Trump's anti-immigration rhetoric and personal appeal? In an election as close as this one, any number of factors could be considered decisive. But we need now turn back to the campaign itself.

3. Did Trump win or Hillary lose or both?

To win, Trump needed not only the Rust Belt voters featured in *The Great Revolt* but also the Main Street conservatives who had been voting Republican for decades. This latter group was probably not a major presence at most Trump rallies. It had no interest in blowing stuff up but fortunately for Trump, it turned out that he could be unconventional as long as he didn't seem irrational, could demonize illegal immigrants so long as he personally didn't reveal himself an out and out racist, and could even rant against globalization and world trade if it would help the cause since there would always be Republicans in Congress to check his worst impulses. It turned out that this group would be willing to overlook an awful lot, including things as basic as temperament, as long as they felt assured that he would nominate pro-business conservatives to the Supreme Court, lower taxes, end Obamacare, cut the size of government and end what they considered needless regulations. Let's look at the wide range of factors that in the end spelled Trump's victory.

a. *The Contract with America*

The elements of Trump's Contract with America announced at his speech in Gettysburg in late October were carefully crafted to appeal both to those who loved the rogue Trump but also to those Republicans who simply needed the reassurance that he would enact a traditional Republican program. It was a comprehensive document and strategically a brilliant stroke.

It began with a list of proposals and actions to eliminate business as usual in Washington, including a constitutional amendment to place term limits on all members of Congress; a hiring freeze on all federal employees, save for the military and those needed to satisfy public health and safety needs; a requirement that each new federal regulation erase two old ones, and a five-year-ban on White House and congressional officials lobbying after leaving government service. Trump then promised five steps "to restore security and the constitutional rule of law," including "canceling every unconstitutional executive action, memorandum, and order issued by President Obama," picking a replacement for Justice Scalia from a pre-approved list of 20 potential nominees, canceling all federal funding to Sanctuary Cities, and suspending immigration from terror-prone regions where the U.S. cannot conduct extreme vetting measures.

After draining the swamp and guaranteeing a conservative Supreme Court if given the chance, Trump moved to a new set of actions "to protect American workers," including scotching restrictions on the production of American energy, including "beautiful clean coal," and giving the green light to the Keystone Pipeline.

Finally, Trump promised to "work with Congress to introduce broader legislative measures including a "massive" tax reduction, the redirection of education dollars to encourage school choice, ending the Common Core, and the full repeal of Obamacare to be replaced by health savings accounts and other initiatives. He also promised the creation of tax-free Dependent Care accounts with matching contributions for low-income families, and the setting of a two-year, mandatory-minimum, federal prison sentence for illegally re-entering America after being deported. He concluded with some major campaign themes, reiterating his pledge to build the wall that Mexico would pay for, withdraw from the Trans-Pacific Partnership, renegotiate NAFTA, raise tariffs to discourage businesses from sending jobs overseas, and declare China a currency manipulator.

Any conservative thinking about not voting for Trump now knew exactly what he would be giving up.

Clinton offered no contract for America or other plainly stated listing of precisely what she wanted to accomplish. Such a document might have been particularly useful in attracting Sanders supporters to her side given the contrast it would draw with Trump. Even a major address delineating her differences with Trump's Contract might have been a bold stroke at a time when almost all the media focus was on the first Comey letter. There is no evidence that the Clinton people ever considered these possibilities.

b. *Make America Great Again*

As noted earlier, Donald Trump trademarked this slogan immediately after the 2012 election. He knew what he was doing. The Democrats seemed not to have understood the strategic value of its message, looking as it did both to the past and the future, committing the candidate to nothing specific but evoking a history on which each voter could project his own meaning. It was a slogan all elements of the party could feel comfortable with. One voter described the impact of the slogan this way: "It was potent and powerful. It takes you to a better place. It's aspirational. And I think Hillary's message Strong Together was flat. It didn't say, come with me" (SZ 171).

In their insightful book, *One Nation Under Trump*, the authors (E.J. Dionne, Norman Ornstein and Thomas Mann) note that the slogan "proved to be a work of political genius" (ED 149). A number of scholars and journalists emphasize how voters could read into the slogan a yearning to return to a white-dominated past. Dionne and his co-authors do not view it so narrowly, seeing in the word "again" an invitation for each voter to view the past in his own light. They agree that for some, "it was a more homogeneous America with fewer immigrants and less pressure to be 'politically correct." But for others, they note, "It was an America of humming factories and productive coal mines when wages were good, Chinese competition was unheard of, unions were strong, and a cottage on a lake was within reach of an average working man" (ED 150).

c. *Hillary's perception problem*

Kellyanne Conway has asserted that female candidates are generally perceived by voters as new and fresh, less corruptible and really good at building consensus. Clinton, however, derived no benefit from these possible generic advantages and, in Conway's words, "the never ending scandalabra of the Clintons butted heads with the 70% of Americans who wanted change." In the end, asserts Conway, Clinton never dented the barrier of the "strong majority of Americans who did not find her honest and trustworthy."

Changing perceptions may have been difficult for Clinton but it may have been a mistake not to try. Voter preferences do swing during the course of a campaign, sometimes in response to events but also in response to changing perceptions of the candidates. Once, for example, Americans decided after their only debate that Ronald Reagan was not the impulsive untrustworthy man portrayed by President Carter, a close election became a rout. It is hard to believe that some of today's voters might not have been similarly subject to persuasion on the issue of her credibility if she had confronted it earlier and more directly. Bill Clinton did go to places that her team would have never sent Hillary, but Bill did not believe he was wasting his time, noting, "You can actually go places where you can make a difference in the vote because people don't expect you to show up there." (AC 333). In the campaign, ABC News estimated that Trump visited Michigan, Wisconsin, and Iowa a total of eighteen times, Clinton went seven times to Michigan and Iowa and zero to Wisconsin (SZ 56).

By not trying to change people's own perceptions about her, Clinton, in my view, played into Trump's hands, allowing him virtually a free hand to batter her with charges of "Crooked Hillary." Whether she liked it or not, she herself was a major issue in the campaign, one that she deliberately chose not to address. It didn't seem to occur to Hillary or her staff that the Obama playbook without Obama might be missing a key ingredient, particularly given that Obama's second victory was not as impressive statistically as the first, especially in the Rust Belt states.

There is no question that the Clinton campaign wanted women to vote their gender. An imaginative campaign might have encouraged this strategy by promoting Hillary's own qualities and showing how they would work to make her an effective President. It was quite amazing to me how the campaign made little attempt to highlight Clinton's good relations with Republicans like John McCain and Bob Gates referred to earlier. Instead, the campaign ran a series of ads aimed at Trump's obvious failings, focusing on his misogynistic remarks and asking women to consider how their own daughters would be affected by the election of such a man.

The ads were effective up to a point as Clinton did outperform Obama among educated white women but they were not effective enough. In the end a majority of white women (53%) supported her opponent. As Kellyanne Conway put it, for many voters, men and women, the issue was not whether they would vote for a woman but whether they would vote for *that* woman. Hillary never figured out a way to stop being "*that* woman" for many and never really tried.

d. *The Pennsylvania itineraries*

Both sides knew that Pennsylvania could be the key to the election and how they scheduled their candidate says a great deal about their overall campaigns.

Though he did deliver a speech to the Union League in Philadelphia — Trump concentrated on smaller cities and towns. He began with a rally at a local high school in Mechanicsburg on August 1. Then he was in Altoona for a rally on August 12; in Manheim on October 1; in Ambridge and Wilkes-Barre on October 10; in Johnstown and Bucks County on October 21; in Youngwood on November 1; in Moon, Harrisburg and Scranton on November 6, and the Lackawanna College Student Union in Scranton on November 7. All told, starting October 1, Trump appeared at ten major rallies in ten different places.

Meanwhile, Hillary's seven events in Pennsylvania were almost entirely devoted to get out the vote type efforts in Pennsylvania's largest cities. Her first visit to Pennsylvania after the Democratic Convention was on August 15 and August 16 when she attended a rally with Joe Biden in Scranton and then the next day did a voter registration rally at West Philadelphia High School. Then she was gone for more than a month. On September 19 she returned to Philadelphia and delivered a speech to students at Temple University. On October 4 she visited Harrisburg and an Environmental Center in Haverford; then on October 22 she was at the University of Pennsylvania in Philadelphia and Taylor Allerdice High School in Pittsburgh; on November 4 she was back in Pittsburgh and the next day she attended a Get Out the Vote Concert with Katy Perry in Philadelphia. She also concluded the campaign with another Get Out the Vote Rally in Philadelphia.

Not once, it appears, did Clinton visit anything approaching a business setting, a church, a small town or rural area. It was as if the Clinton campaign did not even see Pennsylvania as a real place where real people lived in a variety of settings. Rather, for her campaign the state was simply a statistical aggregation of voters and since her voters were primarily in Pittsburgh and Philadelphia, that's where she went. In effect, she left almost the entire state outside its major urban areas to Trump. Much the same could be said of almost the entire country. Clinton rarely campaigned in rural areas and Trump would carry all but 197 counties out of roughly 2100 with a population less than 50,000 (SZ 135).

Would Hillary have won had she scheduled a few rallies outside of Pennsylvania's two major cities? Probably not, but her schedule reflected a larger attitude that might have made the difference in the campaign, including Pennsylvania: safety first, just get out our vote. The voters they did not get out that hurt the most were the younger voters, particularly the millennials (LS 9).

e. *A Republican victory*

Notwithstanding his own estrangement from many G.O.P. leaders, Trump's victory was also very much a Republican victory. They lost only six seats from their large majority in the House and held onto the Senate even though many more of their seats were at risk in the election. They also increased the number of legislatures they controlled from 30 to 32, including a stunning turn-around in the Minnesota State Senate where the party turned a ten-seat deficit into a one seat majority. The only bright spot for the Democrats was in the west where they flipped both houses of the Nevada legislature to their favor and also gained control of the New Mexico House, giving them complete control of the state government.

Three weeks after the election, as it has done for a number of elections, the Kennedy School at Harvard brought together key strategists from both the Trump and Clinton campaigns (as well as strategists for nomination contenders). At the conference, the Trump brain trust acknowledged that Trump would not have won had he not had the intense active support of the Republican National Committee. David Bossie, Trump's Deputy Campaign Manager, acknowledged this debt when he observed:

> The RNC did an amazing job. When I got there late in the campaign in August, we basically dovetailed our efforts with the RNC. We didn't have the time — I didn't have the time — to build it on our own. What they had done over the three years, of building their

modeling and their ground operation, was nothing less than tremendous (Institute 235).

The Republican National Committee's work allowed Trump to preserve the essence of the Republican coalition. Given his personal history and assault on the Republican establishment, this was no mean feat. As Tish Durkin noted in an email exchange, "Trump's rise wasn't that there were white guys in red hats who were eager to inhale heaping helpings of xenophobic demagoguery and half-baked economic populism... It's how many wealthy and/or religious people were thrilled to go right along with them" (TD).

f. *The change agent*

Few would disagree that, as between himself and Hillary Clinton, Trump dominated the campaign and developed the more intense personal following. While very subjective, I would suggest that Trump's victory was also consistent with another pattern, namely, that since the election of FDR in 1932, with perhaps one exception, the presidency has been won by the candidate whose personal qualities seemed to give him the greater advantage.

Certainly, FDR outshone Hoover, Landon, and Dewey (Willkie was probably a draw); Truman's Give 'Em Hell campaign benefited from his no-nonsense everyman personality, abetted no doubt by Tom Dewey's total lack of personal appeal; Eisenhower versus Stevenson was no contest personality wise in the public's mind – the famous "I Like Ike" button emphasizing precisely his edge in that department. John Kennedy's looks, charm and wit and LBJ's overwhelming personality were keys to victory for both men. Jimmy Carter's clear integrity, quiet demeanor and born again Christianity won the entire South for him and was a key to his victory in 1976 after the drama of Watergate. People's view of the Carter persona changed once he became President and he began to seem querulous and even timid, certainly in comparison to the sunny confidence of Ronald Reagan.

Neither George H.W. Bush nor Michael Dukakis had particularly magnetic personalities but Bush had been a war hero in contrast to the famous photograph of Mike Dukakis, his head sticking Ichabod Crane like out of an armored tank, looking more like a joy riding chipmunk than a credible commander-in-chief. Bush ultimately seemed the more appealing figure. Four years later, however, George H.W. Bush was no match in the personality department for Bill Clinton, nor was Bob Dole in 1996; George W. Bush had a relaxed personality that compared favorably to the much stiffer Al Gore and John Kerry. Obama's smile might well have been his most important personal political asset, certainly outshining both Romney and McCain. Humphrey's loss to Nixon was perhaps the only exception to this catalog but the importance of personality in that election was undeniable as Republicans emphasized the new Nixon and Humphrey never quite emerged from the shadow of LBJ to be himself, though he was certainly closing the gap in the last weeks of the campaign.

Of course, personality itself matters most to the extent that it aligns itself with the perceived needs of the moment. In thinking about Trump's victory, no finding is more significant than that 70% of the country believed it was heading in the wrong direction. It is likely that the very same qualities that made many across the political spectrum uncomfortable with Trump as a person — his arrogance, combativeness and incivility — may have also fed into the perception that he was the candidate more likely to create real change.

Put another way, Trump's flaws were more helpful to him than Hillary's virtues were to her.

g. *Hillary's Biggest Mistake?*

Hillary's biggest mistake might have been made eight years before the 2016 election when she decided to give up her U.S. Senate seat to become Obama's Secretary of State. She had been an effective Senator, developing relationships with many Republicans, including social conservatives when she joined the Senate Prayer Breakfast. Elected with 55% of the vote in 2000, she won with 67% of the vote, in 2006, including strong support from rural upstate voters. She even won the praise and endorsement of the two major New York firefighters associations for her role in investigating health issues of first responders to the Trade Center site. Among other things, she forged friendships with key military officials and was able to prevent the closure of several military bases upstate. She led a bipartisan effort to bring broadband access to rural communities. In short, she was a first-rate Senator.

Had she run in 2016 as a distinguished, widely respected U.S. Senator from New York, it would have been a much different election. It is doubtful that she would have anything close to the negative ratings she was saddled with during the 2016 campaign. There would have been no email issue and therefore no Crooked Hillary for Trump to pulverize. As Secretary of State, she had also strongly endorsed the Trans-Pacific Partnership, a position she was ultimately forced to reverse when she was squeezed by the opposition of both Sanders and then Trump who strongly opposed the agreement, as did many rust belt Democratic voters. Her reversal only added to the image of a woman whose sincerity could never be relied upon. Additionally, she would not have been tied to Obama's failed Syria policy or the Benghazi attacks. Moreover, she would not have let her political skills atrophy.

The fact is that for the eight years of the Obama administration she was essentially out of politics, not fighting for people's interests, not confronting the everyday problems and issues of constituents. Instead, she spent four years navigating the world of global politics followed by another four giving speeches to the elite, solidifying her image as a remote and inauthentic figure.

Had she remained a Senator, her political skills would have been at their zenith. In *Shattered*, Allen and Parnes provide a succinct analysis that explains why Hillary and Bill had such different impulses about the election: "For years, she [Hillary] had been in the bubble of the elite circles in Washington, New York, and foreign capitals. Whether or not she understood their concerns, she was literally out of touch with voters. Bill hungered for, and sought, more casual discussions with them" (JA 238). There is more than a little truth to this analysis.

h. *Paula White, Mike Pence, and the Evangelical Vote*

In addition to the Republican Party, Trump owes a great deal to a woman who most people have never heard of. Her name is Paula White, the founder of the Without Walls International Church and a star in the evangelical community. When she came to Donald Trump's attention around 2006, she was preaching to an astonishing 20,000 people a week. They became friends. White went through some bad times but Trump stood by her. She returned the favor by connecting him with key leaders in the religious community, even organizing meetings. The first one in Dallas, Texas in September 2015 involved not only evangelicals but also a Rabbi and a Bishop (SM 94). She reached out to key leaders of the Baptist Community on Trump's behalf as well. At these and other meetings, Trump learned for the first time about the Johnson Amendment that prevented ministers from preaching politics from the pulpit for fear of losing their church's tax-exempt status. When Trump committed himself to its repeal, many decided they were all in with him. Stephen Mansfield, a writer on religion and politics, summed up White's importance this way:

> She prayed for Trump publicly and privately, she gave him counsel, and she helped him win the voters that were certainly among those least likely in all the United States to find him [a] fit. He won by a margin much smaller than the voters she helped draw to him (SM 96).

In 2008 Barack Obama won 26% of the white evangelical vote; in 2012, he won 21%; Hillary won 16% (MW).

Paula White didn't keep evangelicals in the fold by herself. Mike Pence's effectiveness might best be illustrated by what was described as a low-key September event at the Living World Bible Church in Mesa, Arizona. Speaking to about 900 believers, Pence focused on "family faith, and the GOP's shared faith in the American dream." Pence didn't talk a lot about Trump, saying, "All you need to know about Donald Trump is he loves his family, and he loves this country." It was a clever way of linking Trump to conservative social values without going into too much messy biographical detail. Pence did emphasize Trump's German immigrant grandfather and that Trump's father was a self-made man. He also pointed out that a Trump victory would mean lower taxes and a conservative Supreme Court nominee. Did these events matter? They certainly did to some. One young voter at the rally described himself to an Arizona reporter as "up in the air" before the rally but after Pence spoke he said how pleased he was that Pence had chosen to speak at his church and added, "I think I'm going to be going for Trump."

It should not go unnoticed that Trump also owes a considerable debt to Hillary Clinton's campaign strategists for his remarkable share of the Evangelical vote. As Messrs. Dionne, Ornstein and Mann have noted, "Hillary Clinton's campaign was widely critiqued by religious progressives for its failure to organize among religious voters (in contrast to both her own and Barack Obama's 2008 campaigns) and to lift up one of the most authentic and important aspects of Clinton's own persona: the role of her deep religious faith in motivating her progressivism" (ED 232).

i. *The organizations and their strategies*

In her memoir, Clinton acknowledged that the basic strategy was to replicate the Obama coalition and to draw enough suburban republican women to compensate for the expected fall-off in the African-American vote. There really wasn't a comparable grand vision on the other side but certainly Trump's themes themselves created a classic rightwing populist campaign.

In *The Populist Explosion,* John Judis asserts that rightwing populists "champion the people against an elite that they accuse of coddling a third group, which can consist, of immigrants, Islamists, or African American militants... Right-wing populism is triadic. It looks upward, but also down upon an out-group" (JJ 15). In Judis' view, it's the need for an out-group to demonize that distinguishes rightwing from leftwing populism. Trump's message certainly fits easily within Judis's definition of a right-wing populist campaign, the attacks on NAFTA, the "Swamp" in Washington and globalization condemning the elites while all the anti-immigrant and anti-Islamic rhetoric stoked fears of the out-group.

One can't read various insider and other accounts of the campaign without concluding that Trump's campaign advisers were more focused and savvy than Clinton's aides. Clinton's people clearly had a preconceived strategy that they didn't waver from, except perhaps at the end when the late Comey letter forced them to go more negative on Trump than they had planned. Trump's people — perhaps because they knew that their road to victory was narrower — seem to have set the campaign up as a series of challenges, none larger than the 23 to 28 percent of the electorate in each of the key battleground states that thought the country was moving in the wrong direction but had not decided to vote for Trump. At the Harvard Conference, Kellyanne Conway made clear that these were the voters that the Trump people focused on and they broke for Trump in the range of two to one (Institute 178).

Trump's self-confidence was undoubtedly an asset as a candidate. Time and again he would buck the conventional wisdom. Sean Spicer, a political professional who worked for the Republican National Committee during the campaign and served for six months as President Trump's press spokesman, recalls:

> What made the Trump campaign so different was that eight times out of ten they would break the rules and be proven right. We'd say you can't do that, and they would do it anyway. And it would work... and it was also bracing to see a campaign so willing to act indifferently to the sort of political correctness that inhibits all but the most conservative (and

safe-districted) Republican politicians without any apparent cost (SS 92).

Another factor in Trump's favor was an ad campaign that served his needs better than Clinton's did hers. The political scientist Lynn Vavreck studied the television ads of both Trump and Clinton after the election and found that only 9% of Hillary's ads focused on jobs and that more than three-fourths focused on character traits. In contrast, she found that a third of Trump's ads focused directly on the economy. His ads dealing with terror, crime and immigration clearly also were directed at voters looking to change the direction of the country. When one candidate is talking about things that matter to voters and the other candidate isn't, the ultimate result should not be too shocking.

It wasn't as if Clinton didn't have the money to run a more effective campaign. In fact, Hillary out-spent Trump through the whole of the campaign by almost two to one. She and her Super PACs raised and spent roughly $1.2 billion to Trump's roughly $650 million. Their sources were also different. Trump ended up contributing $66 million of his own money to the campaign and received $280 million from small donors giving $200 or less. Hillary received $217.5 million in Super PAC money to Trump's $82.3 million.

Perhaps the most important difference between the two campaigns lay in the kind of information they relied upon to make decisions. The day after Trump's victory, *The Washington Post* carried an article revealing that, anticipating a victory, the Clinton staff was set to reveal that a complex computer algorithm named Ada was the campaign's "invisible guiding hand" (JW). The article went on to say that Ada "was said to have played a role in virtually every decision Clinton aides made," including the deployment of resources. On election night, when Robby Mook, Clinton's campaign manager, reportedly told Hillary that we got the data wrong, he was in effect saying that they got the whole campaign wrong.

It also seems undisputed that the Clinton team, against the wishes of Clinton's pollsters, stopped all state-by-state internal polling in the last three weeks of the campaign. In a later article for *The American Prospect*, Stan Greenberg, Bill Clinton's lead pollster in 1992 and Gore's in 2000, criticized the Clinton campaign's "over-dependence on technical analytics." He also accused the campaign of focusing too much on the rainbow base and identity politics at the expense of the working class. Greenberg found it astonishing that in the last weeks of the campaign, the Clinton team, in his view, "paid little attention to qualitative focus groups or feedback from the field, and their brief daily analytics poll didn't measure which candidate was defining the election or getting people engaged" (SG).

As it turned out, the Trump people had a much better idea of what was happening on the ground than the Clinton people, leading the Trump campaign to pull its advertising in Virginia in the late stages when they determined they couldn't win while Hillary was still looking at possible victories in Iowa and Arizona both of which she lost by wide margins. Hillary had bought completely into the analytics strategy.

Just how much Clinton's people relied on the data, in my view to their detriment, is revealed by a telling anecdote from Amy Chozick's book, *Chasing Hillary*. She relates how Bill Clinton kept trying to convince Hillary's staff that she should accept an invitation to speak at Notre Dame only to be told by Robby Mook that white Catholics weren't the demographic she needed to spend time talking to (AC 235). The point is not that Hillary might have carried Indiana had she gone to Notre Dame. The point is that it would have been a huge event, drawing lots of national media coverage and showing her reaching out to a group not part of her natural constituency.

The key Clinton strategists, stationed as they were in their Brooklyn headquarters, also failed to heed the warnings of those much closer to the battlefronts. Jared Yates Sexton, for example, in his memoir of the campaign, reports how, in the week before November 8, the Service Employees International Union in Michigan "begged to go to work [in Michigan], but the campaign wanted it to serve as a decoy in Iowa. Local operatives were stunned by the lack of attention and focus they received" (JS 257). Sean Spicer recalled in his memoir how crazy it seemed for Hillary to end her campaign in Raleigh, North Carolina with "a high energy get out the vote speech by Lady Gaga" (SS 104), not only because by then it should have been apparent that she would not win there but also because Lady Gaga was "the wrong messenger in the wrong state at the wrong time" (Id).

Clinton's willingness to rely on analytics was clearly linked to her own personality — data after all exudes an aura of certainty that Clinton has always craved — and it also fit with her own belief that she could not convince voters to like her. Very early on in her struggle against Bernie Sanders, Joe Scarborough observed, "Hillary Clinton's problem for people who know her and like her — like I know her and like her — she puts on that political hat, and then she's a robot" (AC 72). Another person who knew it was a problem was Bill Clinton. Amy Chozick reports how Clinton at every opportunity would say to anyone who would listen, "What's the data and organization for if voters don't like Hillary. They need to know the Hillary I know" (AC 175). It was a problem she never overcame, in part possibly because, as I have already emphasized, it was a problem she never really tried to address.

Parenthetically, how did Robby Mook, a thirty-six year old relative newcomer, assume such an important role for Hillary? Amy Chozick reports that the Clintons were extraordinarily impressed with the fact that Mook had managed to help elect their friend, the very non-charismatic Terry McAuliffe, Governor of Virginia in 2013.

Organizational structure was also an advantage for Trump. Larry Sabato has aptly compared Hillary's organization — so "layered with bureaucracy and rival power centers... that it could take a day for everyone to sign off on an innocuous tweet" — with "the always tweeting Trump who cleared his missives with no one" (LS 3). One gets the feeling that decision-making in the Trump camp was a whole lot easier than in Clinton's reflecting, in Sabato's words, Clinton's "ultra-cautious nature and entangling personal alliances" (Id).

j. *Social Media*

Social media was a key part of the Trump strategy. At the Harvard Conference, Brad Parscale, the digital Director of the Trump campaign, noted, "We knew the 14 million people we needed to win 270. We targeted those in 1000 different universes with exactly the things that mattered to them. And we spent the money on digital to do that because we couldn't compete with them on TV" (Institute 229). Parscale added, "Facebook and Twitter helped us win this" (Institute 228). In the end, the Trump campaign used $100 million for its digital outreach and $100 million for TV, a 50/50 split that was unprecedented.

Astonishingly, according to Evan Osnos in his long *New Yorker* piece about Facebook, the Clinton team turned down an offer made to both the Clinton and Trump campaigns to embed Facebook employees for free in their campaigns to help them utilize its platform more effectively in reaching voters. The Trump team accepted the offer, but Clinton's didn't.

Facebook might have proved more valuable than even the Trump campaign expected, for Facebook, according to a *New York Times* article, classified individual voters along the political spectrum (from very conservative to very liberal) and was paid by political campaigns to show their ads to particular groups. According to the article, Trump's campaign paid for ads targeting the politically moderate, an astute choice.

During the campaign, Trump used Facebook to raise two hundred and eighty million dollars. Just days before the election his team paid for a voter suppression effort on the platform. According to Bloomberg *Business Week*, it targeted three Democratic constituencies — "idealistic white liberals, young women, and African-Americans" — sending them videos precisely tailored to discourage them from turning out for Clinton (EO 42).

Twitter was also a major asset to Trump in the campaign. It allowed him to communicate directly with his supporters and also to manipulate the news cycle. Clinton actually posted more tweets than Trump but there is evidence that Trump's were more effective in drawing media attention.

Trump, much more than Clinton, appreciated how radically the infrastructure that shapes our opinions had changed even since 2012. For one thing, Facebook and other social media allowed Trump enthusiasts to create their own synergy, organizing themselves for all kinds of volunteer efforts. It also provided a huge audience for fake news. Buzz Feed's Craig Silverman found that from February through November 2016, fake news stories were viewed close to nine million times, substantially more than the major news stories from mainstream media.

Trump also benefited from what in sports jargon would be called a make-up call where a referee or umpire tries to make up for a bad call against a team by making another questionable call in its favor. Specifically, in his memoir of the campaign, *The People Are Going to Rise Like the Waters Upon Your Shore,* Jared Sexton reports that "Facebook had been exposed in May 2016 for having intentionally stifled conservative trends on the platform" leading in Sexton's view "to an overcorrection in its algorithm that meant the social-media platform was now ripe to serve as an incubator for right-wing news, real or imagined" (JS 255). This in a country where according to a 2016 Pew Survey 62% of its citizens get at least some of their news from social media platforms.

There seems no question that Trump enjoyed the same advantage over Hillary that Obama had enjoyed over McCain eight years earlier. The political scientist Diana Owen has commented on the relative ineffectiveness of Clinton's social media campaign pointing to lost opportunities to simulcast some of best rallies featuring pop-stars like Beyoncé, Jay Z, Lady Gaga, and Katy Perry. She also argues that Clinton's strategy "was aimed at solidifying her base rather than promoting slogans and attracting a larger audience." (DO) She categorized Clinton's social media presence as "nearly invisible" in contrast to that of Trump.

Trump's social media campaign was also aided by the Russian use of fake accounts to infiltrate the internet and promote Trump's prospects. Kathleen Jamieson reports that the Russians posted more than 3500 Facebook ads and that Facebook data shows that the 29 million Americans who directly received Russian Facebook troll posts then relayed them to the newsfeeds of 97 million other Americans for a total reach of 126 million people (KJ 123). Twitter has also released data showing that the Russians used 3,836 Twitter accounts to send nearly 10 million tweets. These accounts had amassed almost 6.4 million followers. In a particularly noteworthy chapter, Jamieson examines how the Russian meddling was designed both to mobilize potential Trump constituencies (veterans and white Christians) and suppress support for Clinton among Sander's supporters, African-Americans, and progressives who might be induced to shift to Jill Stein.

In her important book on the Russian use of cyber-warfare, Jamieson shows how social messaging is particularly effective because, as social science research shows, voters are often persuaded by absorbing the opinions of those they trust (as opposed to mass communications like television advertising), a trait made for a social media world in which friends are constantly posting and re-tweeting to each other. "Facebook," she writes, "is a contagion machine built to order for many good ends but also for fake pages and posts bent on inciting and then harnessing economic anxieties and fears of cultural change" (KJ 48). The book is a primer on what to look out for in 2020. We will be discussing Jamieson's conclusions further in sub-section (p).

k. *The double standard*

One issue that was not mentioned in our story of the campaign was Trump's own ties to Russia. The reason for that was simple: it really didn't become an issue in the campaign and the failure of the media to pursue this story deeply rankled the Clinton campaign. Robby Mook at the Harvard conference asserted:

> There was a sense that Hillary was likely to win this election and, as a result of that, a lot of the treatment in the reporting was

such that if there were something suspicious on the Trump side it would largely go uncovered. But if there was even the slightest suspicion on Hillary's side, it would be blown up quite a bit. In particular, what we found very frustrating was that 17 intelligence agencies claimed that the Russians had stolen the emails from the DNC and stolen the emails from John Podesta, and then a report came out in *The New York Times* that Donald Trump had been under investigation for his connections to Russia…The coverage of what Russian intelligence was feeding to the press versus the deep connections that Donald Trump had with Russia did not get commensurate coverage (Institute 197).

Hillary's staff and she herself, in retrospect, felt that there was a terrible double standard in reporting on the two candidates and that much of the coverage of Hillary was simply in response to things Trump had said. The Clinton people felt that they were never able to figure out how to get sufficient attention paid to her many specific proposals that made her such a superior candidate. While I am very critical of many aspects of Hillary's campaign, I think this charge has some merit. You can't take a selfie with a policy pronouncement. The electronic news media fed off of Trump's tweets and rallies. As CBS President Les Mooves admitted even before Trump won the nomination, "It [Trump's campaign] may not be good for America, but it's damn good for CBS… The money's rolling in and this is fun… It's a terrible thing to say, but bring it on Donald. Keep going." That mentality did not really change even in the general election.

Another interesting "double standard" question is why Trump's huge wealth became a significant part of his appeal to many while Hillary's and Bill's speaking fees were such a liability. It is actually not a difficult question to unpack, for the fact is that Trump's wealth only served to confirm his base's positive impression of him while Clinton's private speeches served to confirm the negative impression of her, particularly among Sanders supporters. Trump's wealth was viewed by his supporters as confirmation of his brains, his business acumen and, perhaps above all, his autonomy. John Jude reports that in the interviews he conducted at Trump rallies, Trump voters invariably praised his self-financing (not entirely true), which was seen as making him independent of special interests and lobbyists. On the other hand, as mentioned, even many Democrats viewed Clinton's Goldman Sachs speeches as proof of her bondage to special interests, an image promoted by Bernie Sanders.

Goldman Sachs' special relationship with the Clintons was actually even closer than most people realized and went back at least two decades. The firm provided some of the Bill Clinton's most influential advisers, contributed to the Clinton Foundation, and leased office space to Bill Clinton. In 2011, with Clinton, as Secretary of State, the State Department endorsed an important Goldman initiative to encourage women entrepreneurship that a *New York Times* article described as central to rehabilitating Goldman's reputation. In an election that was all about change, her Wall Street connections were an important weakness.

1. *The Sanders factor*

One of the things difficult to measure is the impact of the Bernie Sanders primary campaign against Hillary.

In her memoir of the campaign, Hillary has some pretty harsh words for Bernie asserting that his attacks on her as a corporatist were without foundation and that when she challenged him in a debate, he couldn't come up with a single position she had switched as a result of financial contributions from Wall Street. Nevertheless, she argues, Bernie continued to "resort to innuendo and impugning my character" causing "lasting damage, making it harder to unify progressives in the general election and paving the way for Trump's 'Crooked Hillary' campaign." Though she expressed appreciation for his support for her in the campaign, she adds, "He didn't get into the race to make sure a Democrat won the White House, he got in to disrupt the Democratic Party" (HC 229).

As Clinton herself recognizes, in an election as close as 2016, any number of factors can be cited as crucial to the election result. It is clear, however, that she regards Sanders's tactics as an important one. She also admits at various points that she didn't sufficiently reflect in her own speeches and style of campaigning the deep anger that many felt about their own situation.

m. *Why the Billy Bush tape did not sink Trump*

Another question worth pondering more directly is why the Billy Bush tape didn't sink Trump's candidacy. Trump did benefit by the fact that it came out too late for the Republicans to seriously consider removing Trump from the ticket, but Kellyanne Conway might have put her finger on another reason when she later asserted, "There's a difference for voters between what offends you and what affects you."

And there might be something even deeper at work here, something etched into the psyche of many Trump supporters, something at the heart of Arlie Russell Hochschild's book, *Strangers in Their Own Land.*

Hochschild, a University of California, Berkeley sociologist, spent countless hours over a five-year period listening to voters in an arch-conservative parish of Louisiana, one whose economy is dominated by petrochemical plants which dump waste into nearby waters and whose dangerous working conditions created serious health issues for its workers. None of that mattered to many of the area residents she interviewed and got to know, many who were also enthusiastic supporters of the Tea Party. She found, as one might expect, the usual anti-tax, anti-regulation, and anti-liberal sentiments, but more importantly she discerned deeper antagonisms and emotions behind these expressions, what she called "deep stories."

She discovered a group of people that wanted to still believe in the American Dream, but felt that they had been stymied in reaching that goal by an economy that no longer worked for them and by government policies that seemed designed to allow others to cut in front of them, whether the poor who benefited by too generous welfare policies, immigrants taking jobs away, or affirmative action policies unfairly putting them in the back of the line. Then there was the cultural divide, the resentment engendered by the belief that liberals and Democrats looked down on them and were always trying to make them feel guilty and ashamed of who they were.

There is no question that Trump exploited these deeper emotions. A perfect example was provided at a rally in mid-September. Over the previous weekend separate unrelated terrorist attacks had occurred in New York, New Jersey, and Minnesota. Fortunately, no one ended up dead. One attacker, Ahmad Khan Rahami, a 28-year-old naturalized U.S. citizen born in Afghanistan, was being treated for injuries received during his attack in New Jersey. In a

Florida speech, Trump decried that Rahami "will be taken care of by some of the best doctors in the world, he will be given a fully modern and updated hospital room, and he'll probably even have room service, knowing the way our country is." The crowd booed the Trump litany to show that it too shared Trump's outrage. I found the "room service" comment particularly puzzling. Don't all hospital patients get "room service?" Clearly, Ahmad would not be being singled out for special treatment for receiving his food in his hospital room. What Trump knew is that many of those in attendance at his rallies have rarely, if ever, had room service in their lives and that the term evokes a privileged status that an accused terrorist does not deserve.

Notice also that phrase "knowing how this country is." In other words, Trump is reminding his followers, 'this is just one example, I could cite many more.'

Hochschild's subjects rejected the idea that they were homophobic because they opposed gay marriage, racist because they supported the police and opposed affirmative action, that they were anti-immigrant just because they wanted stronger borders and a rooting out of illegal immigrants, that they were stupid simply because they embraced religion. Most of them even rejected environmental regulation, believing that in a choice between regulation and jobs, jobs were by far the most important thing and their only way into a middle class life.

Her book uncovers deep feelings that help explain why even something as obviously embarrassing as the Billy Bush tape would not shift their vote. Democrats who maintain that Hochschild's subjects were duped into voting for Trump should read Hoschild's book. They brought to their support for him the sum total of their life experiences — something that a single bit of tape would hardly overcome.

It is worth mentioning that Hochschild came to admire her subjects, appreciating their "teasing, good-hearted acceptance of a stranger from Berkeley" and noting that the deep stories of both left and right "differ...anchored as they are in biography, class, culture and region." In separate hypothetical letters to her liberal and new conservative friends, she asks the former to "Consider the possibility that in their situation, you might end up closer to their perspective," she asks the latter to try and understand that "you may have more in common with the left than you imagine, for many on the left feel like strangers in their own land too" (AH 233-237).

n. *The third party candidates*

We need to spend a moment on the third party candidacies of Gary Johnson, the Libertarian Party candidate, and Jill Stein, the Green Party candidate. Neither of these candidacies has figured greatly in most of the post-election commentary, but they are worth a brief look. Jill Stein ran to Hillary's left and at one point said that she didn't see much difference between a Clinton victory and a Trump victory. Hopefully, she doesn't still feel that way.

Both Johnson and Stein did much better in 2016 on their respective tickets than they did in 2012, with Gary Johnson going from 1% of the total vote to 3.06% and Jill Stein going from a little more than 0.3% of the total vote to 1.06%. It seems clear that in the absence of a Stein candidacy her voters would have either gone for Clinton or stayed home. The effect of Johnson's candidacy is less clear given that many Libertarians migrated from the Republican Party. It is worth mentioning that, while both Johnson and Stein seemed to hold both candidates in equal disdain, Governor William Weld, Johnson's running mate, made very clear his preference for Clinton over Trump.

Looking at the three rust belt states that determined the election we find that in each state the combined total of the two key third party candidates far exceeded Trump's margin of victory.

Arguably, the third party candidates did make a difference in Michigan, which Trump carried by roughly 14,000 votes and where Johnson received 172,793 votes and Stein 51,420. Putting aside the Johnson candidacy, Stein's vote alone would have been enough to tip the state to Clinton even if half her voters stayed home.

It is less likely (but not at all beyond the realm of possibility) that the third party candidacies made the difference in Wisconsin and Pennsylvania.

It remains a very speculative undertaking given two unknowns: first, how many Johnson and Stein supporters would have stayed home rather than vote for either major party candidate and second, for whom Johnson supporters would have voted. In Wisconsin, Trump won by 27,000 votes over Clinton with Stein garnering 31,000 votes and Johnson 106,292. As for Pennsylvania, Johnson gained 142, 623 votes and Stein 48,998 for a combined total of almost 192,000 votes. Trump, as mentioned carried the State by roughly 44,000 votes. Unlike Florida in 2000, where Nader's third party candidacy clearly affected the outcome of the election, the same cannot be said of the Johnson/Stein efforts in 2016, though it appears likely they made the difference in Michigan, and less likely though not irrefutably so in Wisconsin and Pennsylvania.

o. *The Comey letter*

Another imponderable, one that has been the focus of much attention and speculation, is the effect of the Comey letter late in the campaign. Hillary in her memoir makes clear her belief that it cost her the election. A May 8, 2017 article by Nate Cohn concluded, however, "There's reason to be skeptical of a Comey effect." He pointed to the decline in Hillary's poll numbers in the week preceding the letter, including one that, on the morning of the day the Comey letter was revealed, showed Trump leading in Florida by four points. Much later, on June 14, 2018, Cohn wrote, "it is still unclear" whether the letter cost her the presidency.

Nate Silver, on the other hand, in an article published May 3, 2017, expressed his belief that the letter did probably cost Clinton the election, asserting that "it might have shifted the race by 3 or 4 percentage points to Donald Trump, swinging Michigan, Pennsylvania, Wisconsin and Florida to him, perhaps along with North Carolina and Arizona." But, even if the letter swung the race by just one percentage point, it would, according to Silver, have been enough to elect Trump. Silver does not provide specific evidence for any of the rust belt states and his conclusion is clearly speculative. It is worth pointing out that Pennsylvania did not have early voting so Comey's second letter saying 'never mind' had been issued by the time all Pennsylvanians went to the polls. I'm inclined to Cohn's view that we will never know for sure but certainly the hardest case for saying it swung the election is in Pennsylvania given his larger margin in that state and the absence of early voting.

p. *Did Russia cost Hillary the election?*

In a February 2018 article, Nate Silver described this as one of his least favorite topics in part because its impact is "hard to measure because it wasn't a discrete event." He ends up describing himself as "fairly agnostic" on the question but adds, "Perhaps there are more clever methodologies that one could undertake" particularly "if we knew which states the [Russian] efforts were concentrated on" (NS). Silver did point out, "Thematically, the Russian Interference tactics were consistent with the reasons Clinton lost" and adds, "Would Clinton still have been 'Crooked Hillary' even without the Russians? Almost certainly. But the Russians were at least adding fuel to the right fire — the one that ended up consuming Clinton's campaign" (NS).

Several months after Silver's article, Kathleen Hall Jamieson laid out the case for her belief that the Russian efforts were pivotal to electing Trump. It is a tightly reasoned argument, asserting, among other things, that the hacked materials not only "set in place topics and frames antipathetic to Clinton's interests" but also "primed attributes [alleged hypocrisy and untrustworthiness] damaging to her candidacy." She emphasizes the ways in which matters revealed by WikiLeaks proved particularly harmful during exchanges in the second and third presidential debates that were watched by more than 60 million people (KJ 60). She also describes how the Russian efforts, by reinforcing Trump's messages, helped mobilize his own voters. A particularly telling chapter describes how the Russian efforts might have borne fruit in the last days of the campaign when early voting was occurring and the Comey letter would be having its maximum impact. In an interview with Jane Meyer, Jamieson acknowledged that an "airtight case" could probably never be made but cited the legal standard of "preponderance of the evidence" as being met by what she had discovered. When asked by Mayer point blank whether Trump would be President without the aid of the Russians, Jamieson delivered an unequivocal "NO" (JM).

Like all good scientists, however, Jamieson presents factors that might potentially cast a shadow over her own claim, acknowledging "the short-term nature of most effects, the existence of impervious audiences, and campaigns characterized by counterbalanced amounts of messaging" (KJ 53). Though her book makes a strong case for how voters might have been influenced by Russia's intervention in the campaign — one I can't nearly do justice to in this brief consideration — she also pinpoints precisely the reason that neither she nor anyone else can offer positive proof of its effects, for "we have no good way to isolate the effects of troll-generated and hacked content from the impact of multiple other sources and forms of electoral communication" (KJ 208). This is particularly true, she notes, for those potential voters who chose not to vote as there are no exit polls for non-voters.

I would simply add one other thought. Even if it could be proved beyond a reasonable doubt that Russian interference swung the election to Trump, there is also no way of knowing whether a different, better campaign by Clinton might have saved her from her fate. Let me underscore, however, the importance of Jamieson's work for it lays bare exactly how social media can be hijacked by foreign governments for their own purposes.

q. *A few other factors*

Let me just add a few more observations that I think are important for a fuller picture of the election and then conclude with a final look at the Rust Belt states.

First, one of Clinton's key advantages, the conventional wisdom assumed, in predicting a Clinton triumph, was the huge discrepancy in her favor in the number of offices in the field. But at the Harvard conference, Brad Parscale made a very important point that even Robby Mook, Clinton's campaign manager, agreed with:

> What the RNC did in partnership with
> us — by using the i-Phone and the Android
> devices where you walk out the door and you

could start knocking doors — meant that we didn't need a centralized location. With our budget, it didn't make sense for us to make all those offices so that they could sit there with the door closed. That's a big change. The press was saying we don't have a ground game because we don't have as many offices. That was a dumb argument and one thing the media got wrong about the ground game (Institute 235).

Second, we need to consider the extent to which President Obama must accept some blame for the 2016 result. In a column shortly after the election, Maureen Dowd argued that Obama never understood the greater meaning of his own victory in 2008: "Voters waited in line for hours at those [Obama's] early rallies because they wanted thunderous change. They wanted a newcomer who didn't look like the old dudes on our money, someone who would bust up the incestuous system and give us, as the poster said, hope." I agree that Obama never really channeled or fully appreciated the nation's anger over what had happened in 2008. Not a single banker was ever convicted or even charged in connection with the massive failures that ruined so many lives. By comparison, the much less serious savings and loan crisis of the 1980s produced more than 800 indictments.

Dowd's criticism of Obama also came to mind when I read a March 2017 article in the *New Republic* by Michael Sifry. The article describes how the grassroots machine of two million supporters that Obama built in the 2008 campaign was essentially demobilized by the Democratic National Committee after the election (MS). As a result, what had been an independent progressive voice was folded into the structure of the DNC where it sank into oblivion. Obama concurred in this development. Consequently, there was simply no strong, independent voice on the left that Clinton might have used to rally Sanders supporters in the general election.

Third, notwithstanding how disturbing they were, Trump's events were an extremely important part of his strategy. They helped him dominate the news cycle and stoked the enthusiasm of many. As Larry Schweikart notes, "Rally attendees were more likely to volunteer, staff phone banks, tell neighbors, and so forth" (LS). Moreover, as stated earlier, the rallies were huge local news creating many opportunities for local television and radio interviews, affording Trump the opportunity to bypass the unfriendly commentary of cable television's talking heads (JP 177). His rallies created a cottage industry for t-shirts, buttons, hats, and other campaign apparel and paraphernalia. The coverage the rallies received was extraordinary. At the Harvard conference, one of Clinton's advisers recalled how the cable networks would build up the anticipation for a Trump rally by actually fixing for minutes at a time on an empty hall before the actual event. I saw this myself on numerous occasions.

It should be noted that Trump held many more rallies than Clinton. NBC News estimated that Trump spent 50% more time than Clinton in the six key battleground states of North Carolina, Ohio, Florida, Pennsylvania, Michigan, and Wisconsin.

Finally, though I have criticized Clinton for an unimaginative, run out the clock campaign, fairness requires an acknowledgement that, according to realclearpolitics.com, Clinton led in 155 of the 182 national polls taken between June 1 and Election Day, the outliers primarily being those conducted by The Los Angeles Times and Rasmussen Reports. There was, therefore, nothing in the national polls that might have alerted her to the need for some rethinking of her basic strategy.

r. *A closer look at the Rust Belt states*

In the end, Clinton would have won the presidency had she won Pennsylvania, Wisconsin, and Michigan, so in a sense the question did Hillary win or Trump lose comes down to a question of how these three states ended up in the Trump column.

Trump won Pennsylvania by roughly 44,000 votes. In Pennsylvania, Clinton actually improved on Obama's margin of victory in the Philadelphia suburbs of Bucks, Chester, Delaware, and Montgomery Counties. Obama won them by a margin of 123,327; she won them with a margin of 179,464. Her margin in Philadelphia was slightly less than Obama's 2012 margin but not by a lot. Obama carried the City by 492,339, Hillary by 455,124. Philadelphia and its suburbs gave Hillary a margin of 634,000 votes. Had Trump only matched Romney's margin of 305,826 outside the major urban areas, Trump would have lost Pennsylvania by a wide margin. He won instead because his margin throughout most of the rest of the state was 702,490, more than doubling Romney's. Trump's better showing wasn't confined to rural Pennsylvania. Erie County, for example, once a major manufacturing center but now where factories stand empty, went from supporting Obama by a margin of 19,000 votes to supporting Trump by almost 2,000 votes. It is hard to resist the conclusion that the key to Trump's victory in Pennsylvania was the overwhelming turnout and support he received in the rural areas and small cities and towns in the rest of the state and that in turn represented a real personal triumph for him and his strategists for whom Pennsylvania was the key to the election.

There is, however, always more than one way of looking at things. An article on Bloomberg.com by Albert Hunt claims that "Clinton Lost Pennsylvania More than Trump Won It" pointing out among other things that in Philadelphia there were almost 100,000 fewer voters than in 2012. And Hunt is correct. Clinton won roughly 85% of the vote in Philadelphia so with an additional 100,000 voters she would have gained an additional 70,000 votes, significantly more than Trump's 44,000 vote margin of victory. But was it really likely that Clinton could achieve the same turnout in 2016 as Barack Obama had in 2012? However one wants to look at it, the fact remains that Trump persuaded lots of people to change their vote from Obama to himself, for example, winning Lackawanna County by a small margin after Obama had carried it by almost 17 percentage points in 2012, and making inroads in places like Scranton, which Obama had won by 16 points in 2012. Northampton County which takes in much of the Lehigh Valley was another important county that switched from Obama to Trump.

In Wisconsin, more than Pennsylvania, it appears that low Democratic turnout may have been the reason for the Clinton loss. In Milwaukee County, for example, the most populous in the state, Clinton received approximately 289,000 votes to Obama's 328,000, a difference of 39,000 votes in a State she only lost by 27,000. Total turnout was down among Democratic and Republican voters by roughly 240,000 voters. It is hard to resist the conclusion that Clinton's failure to ignite real enthusiasm among Democratic voters was the main culprit of her defeat in Wisconsin, a not surprising outcome when you consider that she never once stepped foot in the state during the campaign, a fact perhaps not forgotten by the 14% of Wisconsin voters who did not make up their minds until the last week of the campaign and who broke for Trump 59% to 30%.

In Michigan, the story appears to be both about voter turnout and Trump's strong appeal. Clinton lost Michigan by roughly 14,000 votes. Had she carried Wayne County (Detroit) by anything like what Obama had done in 2012, she clearly would have won the state. Instead, she received 84,000 fewer votes than Obama. Even then, however, she would have won but, unlike Wisconsin, Trump garnered 160,000 more votes than Romney.

In a March 28, 2017 article for *The New York Times*, Nate Cohn concluded that though turnout played a modest role in Mr. Trump's victory, "the big driver of his gains was persuasion: He flipped millions of white working-class Obama supporters to his side." In the Midwestern battleground states and Pennsylvania, Clinton lost a full 20% of Obama supporters to Trump.

Cohn's analysis is strengthened by a demographic chart appearing in a February 23, 2017 article by Nate Silver showing the estimated percentage of White Non-College voters in each of the swing states. With the exception of a couple of outliers, the swing states with the higher proportion of white non-college voters went for Trump. White non-college educated voters made up 53% of Michigan's electorate, 57% of Wisconsin's, 62% of Iowa's, 53% of Ohio's, and 50% of Pennsylvania's. On the other hand, the swing states that went for Hillary, with the exception of New Hampshire, all had a much lower proportion of white non-college voters: Nevada's was 42%, Colorado also 42% and Virginia 37%. Though Florida and North Carolina both have a low percentage of white non-college voters (40%), Trump's victories in those states can be largely explained by the million plus Cuban Americans in Florida and the fact that North Carolina has been a traditionally Republican state, the one state that flipped from Obama to Romney in 2012.

* * *

Was Trump's success inevitable? Could a different strategy on Clinton's part have made a difference? It is certainly conceivable that a more imaginative, slightly braver campaign might have put Clinton over the top in the three rust belt states that she lost by a margin of three-tenths of 1%(Michigan), 1% (Wisconsin), and 1.2% (Pennsylvania). It certainly didn't help that, according to the Wesleyan Media Project, Clinton did not begin advertising in either Michigan or Wisconsin until the last week of the campaign (DC 9). Given that a full 55% of the public thought Clinton had the right temperament for the presidency compared to barely a third who thought the same about Trump, might not she have found a better way of exploiting this advantage rather than focusing on Trump's negatives, which frankly needed no pointing out? Could she not have rallied the nation around a few thematically linked national commitments?

New York Times columnist David Brooks has tried to explain Donald Trump's appeal this way:

> The story Donald Trump tells is that we good-hearted, decent people of Middle America have been betrayed by stupid elites who screw us and been threatened by foreigners who are out to get us. That story resonated with many people.

And then Brooks concludes:

> You can get a lot of facts wrong if you get your story right. (DB at A21)

If one sentence can succinctly summarize the entire 2016 campaign, it is probably this last one, for Trump clearly had a story to tell — a story with heroes, all the unsung voters who would become heroes by letting Trump rescue them, and villains, all the politicians of both parties and the global elite they served. The big metropolitan areas had largely recovered from the Great Recession but many rural areas and smaller cities, most importantly in the Rust Belt, had not. Unlike Trump, Hillary had facts but no story. Breaking the glass ceiling was a theme, not a story. Breaking it would bring back no jobs, nor would it put bread on the table or assuage the deep resentments that drove so many to her opponent. Above all, perhaps, Trump, the businessman ironically knew something that Hillary, the seasoned politician, didn't.

The American novelist Ursula K. Le Guin has written:

> Words are events, they do things, change things. They transform both hearer and speaker; they feed energy back and forth and amplify it.

In the battle of the narratives, Trump won by default. His words became events. Hers did not. It hurts to say it. But he was the more effective candidate.

Part II: Today and Tomorrow

Chapter 3

Where we are now

1. Thinking About Trump.

Donald Trump is unprecedented. We have never had a President perceived by many intelligent and rational people as a threat to our very system of government. Harvard Law Professor, Michael Klarman, has asserted "President Trump poses a greater threat to the rule of law than anything Americans have witnessed in a generation" (MK). Klarman cites examples ranging from Trump's penchant for punishing corporate executives who have dared to defy him to his attacks on the press and constant questioning of the integrity of the election process, with much in between. It has had its effect. One Gallup poll showed 52% of Republicans saying they would support Trump if he called for a delay in the next presidential election on some claimed necessity. Since early April 2019, the date of Klarman's writing, President Trump has decided to wage his own war with the Democratic-held House, refusing to cooperate in any way with its investigation of him or his administration in the exercise of Congress's oversight role.

Five days after 9/11, President George W. Bush exhorted America not to condemn all of Islam and all Muslims after visiting the Islamic Center in Washington, D.C.:

> The face of terror is not the true faith of Islam. That's not what Islam is all about......
> Muslims are doctors, lawyers, law professors, members of the military, entrepreneurs, shopkeepers, moms, and dads. And they need to be treated with respect... Moms who wear head cover must not be intimidated in America. That's not the America I know. That's not the America I value... Those who feel they can intimidate their fellow citizens to take out their anger don't represent the best of America, they represent the worst of humankind, and they should be ashamed of that kind of behavior.

Can anyone even begin to imagine Donald Trump uttering these thoughts — the man who claimed that Muslims in Jersey City jumped for joy at the collapse of the World Trade Center?

Trump has been anything but a normal President and some urged from the start not to normalize him.

As understandable as that may have been, supporters normalized him when there were enough of them (though three million fewer than his opponent) to make him the President of the United States. His election and his conduct of the Presidency must be examined as we would any other President. Failure to do so, failure to try and place the meaning of his election and his choice of policies in historical context, is an invitation to disaster both for those who oppose him and for those who simply want to understand our own politics a little better.

There is a difference between a bad President and an illegitimate one. Against his own predictions, Trump won a non-rigged election.

Stephen Skowronek in his *Presidential Leadership in Political Time* gives us a path for contextualizing the Trump presidency. Skowronek has proposed that presidential leadership over the course of our history has fallen into what he calls "regimes," each regime representing a period in what he calls "political time," hence the title of his book.

Each regime — he identifies five — begins with the election of a transformative President — Jefferson, Jackson, Lincoln, FDR and Reagan — by the vote of "an insurgent coalition" that marks the end of the prior regime. Within each regime period, Presidents not of the party of the transformative President are elected. They do not alter the basic nature of the prevailing regime because they do not govern in a way that alters its basic commitments. For example, neither Grover Cleveland's nor Woodrow Wilson's victories during the regime (1860-1932) of "Republican nationalism" (Skowronek's phrase) altered in Skowronek's view the fundamental ethos of the Republican nationalism regime. While warning that frameworks like his own cannot be viewed too mechanistically, Skowronek also suggests that the presidencies immediately preceding those of the transformative Presidents — we are speaking here of John Adams, John Quincy Adams, James Buchanan, Herbert Hoover and Jimmy Carter — represented to some degree a last gasp of the prior regime, signaling its growing weakness.

In an essay on President Obama, written only two years into his first term, Skowronek tried to assess where Obama might fit into his framework, an obviously speculative task at that point. In reading the essay I was struck by the following brief passage:

> With the Republican Party prodded on by the Tea Party movement, the prospect cannot be ruled out that Obama's presidency will serve to propel the conservative movement forward toward a final, more decisive rout of the progressive alternative. A passing thunder on the Left might be just the thing to catalyze a second and more thoroughgoing reconstruction from the Right (SS188).

Skowronek has asserted — correctly I believe — that the conservative ascendancy inaugurated by Reagan's presidency was not as thoroughly transformative as earlier regimes because in some ways it did not attack the basic programmatic commitments of the liberal era. The passage quoted above was leaving open the possibility that the conservative triumph of 1980 needed a further impetus to realize its ambitions and suggests that Obama's presidency might actually produce that reaction.

Do we see the realization of that speculation in Trump? I would argue that Trump has represented, if nothing else, a "thoroughgoing reconstruction from the Right" but in ways so unpredictable that traditional definitions of conservatism are no longer applicable. Coupled with his unorthodox — the most neutral term I can think of — approach to governance, might Trump, if re-elected, properly be seen as a transformative President?

Certainly, Trump's victory in 2016 can be seen as the triumph of an "insurgent coalition." Many at Trump's rallies, though admiring Trump personally, also emphasized that he was the beginning of a whole new force in American politics and remember how the many volunteers who organized themselves into teams and even purchased billboard space stunned Trump's professional operatives. But has Trump's presidency constituted a thorough going "reconstruction from the Right?"

In one sense, the answer is clearly no. After all, just like Reagan, the major accomplishment of Trump's first two years was a huge, deficit enlarging tax cut. Like Reagan, he also has placed a premium on de-regulation. So, for all his rhetoric, he has in some ways done exactly what you might expect a normal Republican to do. Moreover, many of the aspects of his presidency that most disturb voters, even some of his supporters, are so personal to him that it is questionable whether they will constitute any kind of legacy in Skowronek's framework.

Yet it is hard to imagine Trump not being seen as a transformative president if he is re-elected given the way he has chosen to govern, for he has stood on its head the presidency's most "basic governing commitment: that the President be seen as governing on behalf of all the people and not just those who elected him. In his first inaugural address Thomas Jefferson, famously proclaimed "We are all Republicans, [and] we are all Federalists." He was trying to remind the country of its commitment to common principles after a campaign that, at least until 2016, set the gold standard for nastiness.

In contrast, Trump's governing style is closer to the royalist claim, "I am the State," his nation synonymous with his supporters.

Trump's inaugural address makes interesting reading in light of his subsequent presidency. When I saw him deliver it along with tens of millions of others, it seemed more like a campaign speech. Certainly, there were some of the same themes. Almost as if he was addressing his base alone, for example, he trashed the Washington establishment: "Their victories have not been your victories. Their triumphs have not been your triumphs." And he spoke of a deeply dysfunctional nation evoking "mothers and children trapped in poverty in our inner cities, rusted out factories, scattered like tombstones across the landscape of our nation, an education system flush with cash, but which leaves our young and beautiful students deprived of all knowledge, and the crime, and the gangs, and the drugs that have stolen too many lives and robbed our country of so much unrealized potential." And then, in perhaps the most memorable line in the speech, he added, "This American carnage stops right here and stops right now."

Yes, these were themes – it turns out effective themes – we all recognized, but what also emerges is how completely Trump saw himself then, presumably still now, as a transformative president, transformative in a very specific way, for, to his supporters, he would restore American nationalism to its rightful place: "We assembled here today are issuing a new decree to be heard in every city, in every foreign capital, and in every hall of power, from this day forward: a new vision will govern our land, from this day forward, it's going to be only America first. America first." And then again: "At the bedrock of our politics will be a total allegiance to the United States of America, and through our loyalty to our country, we will rediscover our loyalty to each other."

What I had forgotten was the way the address tied his theme of a greater unity for all the people of the nation to an idealized nation of racial unity. Consider this passage: "A new national pride will stir our souls, lift our sights and heal our divisions. It's time to remember that old wisdom our soldiers will never forget, that whether we are Black, or brown, or white, we all bleed the same red blood of patriots. We all enjoy the same glorious freedoms, and we all salute the same, great American flag. And whether a child is born in the urban sprawl of Detroit or the windswept plains of Nebraska, they look up at the at the same night sky, they fill their heart with the same dreams and they are infused with the breath of life by the same almighty creator." Could not Robert Kennedy have spoken those words?

How stillborn those words sound today. We have never had a President whose most basic instinct is to divide people. His constant Tweeting on all sorts of matters that no previous President would even think of addressing; his war on the press, declaring it the enemy of the people; the tone of his rhetoric that has certainly made white supremacists feel that they may have an ally in the White House; his refusal to accept the intelligence findings of his own government; and his never-ending effort to demonize whomever disagrees with him; all attest to a fundamental abandonment of standard presidential behavior. And few would deny that this President simply continually misrepresents facts and makes assertions that are demonstrably untrue.

All transformative presidents in Skowronek's terms have been easily re-elected (Lincoln's was the closest race) and so too must Trump to merit similar status. It is what makes 2020 such a pivotal election. If defeated, Trump would become only the third sitting President since the beginning of the Great Depression to be beaten in a general election. If the newly-elected Democratic President is successful in enacting progressive policy proposals – undoubtedly a Democratic Senate would also be needed — we may well have begun a new "regime" in Skowronek's terms. In that event, Trump would be following historically in the footsteps of Carter, Buchanan, and Hoover.

2. We've Been Here Before.

It is well to remember that we have been here before. At the beginning of the twentieth century, the nation was grappling with enormous challenges not dissimilar to our own. Today we grapple with how Amazon, Google, and Facebook may be dominating our lives, but similar concerns were earlier evoked by United States Steel, Standard Oil, American Tobacco, and many other trusts at the turn of the century. Then too, the huge influx of Catholics and Jews from Eastern Europe caused many to fear that the American way of life was in peril, fears echoed by the many Trump voters who spoke of feeling strangers in their own country. Income inequality as early as 1890 was so pronounced that a Republican ex-President Rutherford B. Hayes confided to his diary that the "The wrongs and evils of the money-piling tendency of our country" were bringing "all power to the rich" and resulting in "pauperism and its attendant crimes and wretchedness like a flood." Our top 1% has nothing on the top 1% of 1900 when there was no income tax at all.

As also the case today, early twentieth century reformers questioned whether existing institutions were up to the task of meeting the problems of the day. In the early 1900s, this feeling led to many innovations on the state level, including direct legislation by the people through the initiative process, the right to recall elected officials, and nominations through a primary system. During this period, three constitutional amendments, providing for an income tax, the direct election of Senators, and a woman's right to vote, were ratified.

Today we worry that partisan and incumbent gerrymandering has created a system where legislators choose their voters instead of voters choosing them, a system where the kind of common-sense solutions that a vast majority of Americans could embrace are precluded by a political system that simply no longer represents their view. This is a system marked by the need for elected officials to be constantly begging for money from the very special interests they are supposed to regulate, all at the expense of the public interest. Indeed, the very idea of the "public interest" seems rather quaint, a product of an earlier time. It is a phrase simply not used much anymore.

Every generation tends to think its problems are unique but it is remarkable how today's debates are simpler newer versions of issues we have been confronting our entire history. Today's arguments over immigration are just the latest chapter in the effort to define who we are as a people and what we represent. There are periods in our history where we have been welcoming and some when we were not so welcoming but the continuing debate is fundamental to our identity. The controversies over the individual mandate in the healthcare law and over gun control are simply the latest versions of the never-ending debate over society's right to legislate in the public interest at the expense of individual freedom of behavior. President Trump's obvious distrust, even disdain, for internationalism is simply his answer to a question we have been debating since the end of the nineteenth century about America's proper role in the world. The progressive agenda of universal health care and tuition free college education once again asks us to consider just how robust our social safety network should be, hardly a new question. We have been arguing over the use of federal lands, the proper sphere of regulation, how much respect to afford individual conscience, the proper balance between state and federal powers, government's responsibility for mitigating poverty and inequality, how best to educate our children, what separation of church and state actually requires, and many other issues for most of our history.

The continuity of our issues may bespeak an underlying strength.

What seems to be different now is a feeling that there is nothing on the other side worth considering. Not only is this attitude dangerous in a democracy, it ignores the simple fact that the two major parties, from the New Deal through the balance of the twentieth century, did stand for two healthy instincts, one emphasizing the role of the private sector, the other the role of government, in solving our problems. When we ignore each other, as we may be doing now, we ignore finding the best solutions to our problems.

We do have one great strength that we rarely talk about.

I refer to our system of federalism, a structure fundamental to the success of our now more than 225 history of self-government. It not only allows us to experiment with various solutions to national problems at lower levels — think, for example, healthcare under Romney in Massachusetts that became a virtual model for Obamacare — but it plays a major role in allowing public opinion to change slowly over time. In our unique federal system, important political battles can be fought out in fifty separate arenas. The gay rights movement changed attitudes about gays slowly over decades through battles waged state-by-state, locale after locale. Both sides, of course, can use these tactics. The pro-life movement has been waging a guerilla war against abortion in a huge swath of states just as progressives fight at the state and city level for higher minimum wages and gun control.

The great conservative Supreme Court Justice, John Marshall Harlan III, thought the key protection for individual rights lay in our federal system, in the way it diffused power and left much for the states to decide. We just saw a recent example when 45 states, Republican and Democratic, refused to comply with the request of the Advisory Commission on Electoral Integrity, a Trump creation, for detailed information on individual voters. The Commission was ultimately allowed to die.

It isn't just about how states diffuse political conflict. County and city governments are crucial in shaping the fabric of American life. Local civic pride and community involvement fuel progress and creativity that rarely gets recognized in the national media. For five years starting in 2013 James and Deborah Fallows visited forty-two towns in every region of the country, speaking with newspaper editors, visiting bars, chatting up anyone who looked interesting, finding out about local history, and how these towns were facing the future. At the end of their journey, the Fallows recalled the words of Philip Zelikow, Professor at the University of Virginia, who at the beginning of their travels had told them:

> In scores of ways, Americans are figuring out how to take advantage of the opportunities of this era, often through bypassing or ignoring the dismal national conversation. There are a lot more positive narratives out there – but they're lonely and disconnected. It would make a difference to join them together, as a chorus that has a melody.

"This," the Fallows conclude, "is the American song we have heard" (DF 400).

In the balance of this chapter, I want to address two matters: first, how the revival of the kind of consensus encouraging politics I seek requires the support of our electronic media and second how a willingness to consider centrism in a new light, not as some mythical middle ground, but as a different approach to politics itself, may be a key to the kind of consensus politics that I believe a majority of Americans still want.

3. Making the Clash of Ideas Work for All of Us

In his inaugural address, President Kennedy reminded us that "civility is not a sign of weakness and sincerity is subject to truth." Insults and personal attacks should not be confused with genuine debate which expose you to the possibility that you may be wrong, or at least that there is validity to other viewpoints.

Judge Learned Hand once wrote:

> The spirit of liberty is the spirit which is not too sure it is right; the spirit of liberty is the spirit which seeks to understand the minds of other men and women; the spirit of liberty is the spirit which weighs their interest alongside its own without bias...

Unfortunately, our new media world seems designed to exacerbate our worst instincts and move us even further from Hand's vision. Today we have become not only political partisans but media partisans as well. Watching a non-friendly station can seem almost like a betrayal. One woman told Arlie Hochschild, "Fox is like family to me... Bill O'Reilly is like a steady, reliable dad. Sean Hannity is like a difficult uncle who rises to anger too quickly. Megyn Kelly is like a smart sister..." (AH 126).

This rise of the politicized media has grown almost exactly in tandem with the growth of the internet. In an interesting podcast, Stanford professor Shanto Lynegar, quoted earlier, noted, "The media market has changed quite profoundly in the aftermath of the IT revolution," creating an internet marked by a multiplicity of news sources, many catering to a particular ideological perspective. Lynegar also describes how the rapid success of Fox News in establishing itself as the No. 1 rated news source "told producers, people contemplating entering the media market as providers, that there was sufficient demand for biased news" (SL).

It used to be that the major job of the traditional electronic media was to report the news in a way that allowed people to come to their own conclusions about the day's events. Today, it seems that its major function is to sort us out in ways that improve its own bottom line without regard to the damage it may do to rational debate in the process. One Trump supporter from Luzerne County complained, "It's tough to get objective, non-biased reporting these days" (BB 81).

In an increasingly competitive media environment, cable networks must be conscious of what their audiences want. That, however, is not usually the stuff of what helps voters make informed decisions. The researcher and author, Marjorie Hershey, has perceptively written:

> To survive, then, media people try to learn what their prospective audience wants to see covered in the news. They develop a definition of "news" based primarily not on the democratic citizen's need to know but on the media's need to gain an audience (MH 114).

And, she adds, "...detailed discussions of the most vital and complex issues of governance are a one-way ticket to ratings hell" (Id). Could this kind of environment have been any less conducive to Hillary's needs or more attuned to Trump's?

If the political center disappears it may be because it is not an appealing demographic for an electronic media for which news is simply the raw material for vindicating its political point of view.

Rachel Maddow, Lawrence O'Donnell, Don Lemon, Sean Hannity, Laura Ingraham, and all the other partisan commentators generally try to portray the other ideological side in the worst possible light, not just misguided but dangerous. There is no doubt a connection between the growing disregard that each side has for the other and what they see on television every day.

A good friend criticized a draft of this last paragraph for seemingly equating Fox's dignifying of Trump's falsehoods with MSNBC's effort to combat them. My point, however, is not that there is a moral equivalence in their messages but that they both are in the business of serving their separate audiences. I might prefer Maddow, O'Donnell, and Lemon but night after night they would latch on to the slightest bit of information suggesting collusion between the Trump campaign and the Russians as if there was almost nothing else going on in the world.

It is a shame. The country deserves better. I'm reminded of the night toward the end of the 2016 campaign when I went to a public conversation between Peter Singer, the controversial ethicist, and Robert George, a very conservative but extremely popular (among all shades of opinion) political science professor at Princeton. In the Q and A, the subject of Trump came up and Professor George noted that he was from West Virginia and went back there often and that it was as hard to find a Clinton supporter in his part of West Virginia as it was to spot a Trump sign in Princeton. A Hillary supporter then asked a question that implied negative things about anyone who supported Trump and George responded that the people he talked with in both places were fundamentally decent and well-meaning with their views reflecting their own experiences and problems. And, of course, he is correct. Indeed, if you don't believe in the fundamental decency of most people and if you don't recognize that decent people can look at the world very differently, there is not much point in having a democracy.

It portends real danger for democracy when there is simply no one deemed worthy of the public's trust. Walter Cronkite was important not just because people trusted him but because they trusted the whole system of reporting and dissemination he represented.

A presidential election should have a cleansing effect. We have taken our national temperature, chosen our only nationally elected leaders, and hopefully thrashed out some issues. But that is no longer what happens. Mario Cuomo famously said that we campaign in poetry but govern in prose, except that, in an era of 24/7 politics, there seems little room or appetite for prose.

It would help if the electronic media could expose the average voter to something better than dueling sound bites on the critical issues facing the country. That role becomes particularly acute at a time when social media allows each of us to live in our own comfort zone where friends talk only to friends. The electronic media should be helping break down barriers, not build them up.

Late in the 2016 presidential campaign, the Center for Disease Control and Prevention published a study revealing that in 2014 the suicide rate for children aged 10 to 14 had caught up to the death rate due to traffic accidents. If you had asked me how many American children aged 10 to 14 actually killed themselves in 2014, I would have guessed something in the neighborhood of 50, which is still roughly one a week. It turns out the number is 450, meaning that adolescent boys and girls are killing themselves at a rate greater than one a day. Neither the media

— nor therefore the candidates — gave the report the time of day

In my journal entry for September 30, 2016, I tried to capture the contrast between what the media was focusing on in the presidential campaign and what was happening in the rest of the world. I wrote:

> So here, right now, is what preoccupies the electronic media: was Donald Trump, when a private citizen, for or against the Iraq War before it began? Did Hillary Clinton help Alicia Machado — the Miss Universe winner whom Trump denigrated after she gained weight — get her citizenship? Did foreign governments give Hillary millions of dollars as alleged by Trump's campaign manager? Did Donald Trump do business with Cuba at a time when it was illegal? Which is worse, that Trump married three times or that Hillary married only once? Whose foundation has worse conflicts of interest?
>
> Meanwhile, here are just a few of the things that have been happening on Planet Earth:
>
> Women and children in Aleppo are being buried alive courtesy of Russian carpet bombs. North Korea has successfully tested a ballistic missile, aiming to have one in the near future that can reach the continental United States. Iran and Saudi Arabia continue to wage a proxy war in Yemen creating untold misery. The Philippines, in pursuit of better relations with Russia and China, will no longer conduct joint military exercises with the United States military. India has launched a surgical strike

on Pakistani militants following the killing of 18 Indian soldiers in the Kashmir in February 2019. Thousands of Haitian refugees are stranded at the American border as the United States reverses its policy on accepting Haitians lacking visas. Further, it is now official — the world has just experienced the hottest summer in recorded history. Meanwhile, at home, wages remain virtually flat for 90% of Americans as they have for decades while the wealthiest 1% of Americans have seen their income approach levels that might have made Midas blush. A recent survey by the Federal Reserve showed that close to a majority of Americans would not be able to handle an unexpected emergency expense of $400 from cash reserves. Annual deaths from drug over-doses now exceed the total number of soldiers who died in the entire Vietnam War.

During the campaign, CNN had a running visual show-ing the countdown to the next debate right down to the minute, exactly as sports channels do for the Super Bowl.

Justice Oliver Wendell Holmes believed in free speech but only because in the marketplace of ideas, the truth would have the best chance to emerge. But what if there is no marketplace? A marketplace is where people meet and ideas are exchanged and evaluated. It is common ground. Metaphorically, it's the place where free speech can do its work, where attitudes can change. A segregated media can no longer perform that function — it is no longer a marketplace. Indeed, even those most consumed by today's politics rarely talk to each other. Consider this observation by David Brooks:

> Over the past month {July 2019}...I at-
> tended four conferences. Two were very
> progressive, with almost no conservatives.
> The other two were very conservative, with
> almost no progressives. Each of the worlds
> was so hermetically sealed I found that I
> couldn't even describe one world to members
> of the other. It would have been like trying to
> describe bicycles to a fish (DB).

The election of 2020 will provide a real opportunity
for the media to get it right but it might take the radical
step of Fox News, CNN and MSNBC, for example, talking together to recognize a common problem.

One worthwhile effort would be to get all sides listening
to the same people at the same time. Nothing prevents, for
example, these three networks (and others) from jointly
sponsoring a series of issue forums to be broadcast simultaneously on each channel. There is precedent. I remember
William Buckley's Firing Line debates where three commentators on one side of an issue were arrayed against
three commentators on the other, each making presenta-
tions and then questioning each other. No shouting. It was
just sharp but respectful back and forth. The debate on
the Panama Canal Treaty during the Carter years, which
featured Ronald Reagan among those opposing the treaty,
was a model of what constructive debate can be all about.
There is no better way to see that there are often two sides
(sometimes more) to an issue.

Presidential debates, as presently configured, are not
an effective method for educating voters about issues, first
because they cover such a wide range that none can be
discussed in any but a superficial way. Nor is issue education in any way a purpose of these gladiatorial encounters.
Their purpose is simply to help voters decide for whom

to vote. Each candidate will, of course, define his position on issues but even then only to the extent it aids his or her candidacy. The only contrast that either debate participant cares about is with the other candidate, the only goal to excite one's base and/or attract the support of undecided voters.

Debates today fail on the education front for two other reasons as well: press coverage and social media. Almost invariably media coverage of virtually every debate comes down to looking for one or two decisive moments on which to focus, something dramatic perhaps, or a mistake, or a revealing moment of character or personality. Even if a debate manages to have a few moments of real substance on an issue, it is not likely to be accorded much attention in the wake of the press's real interests.

As for the new world of social media, it has altered the very way many viewers watch debates. Presidential debates are now a social media event as a result of something called "dual screening," meaning watching an event and simultaneously twittering or engaging with others about it in real time. One study of the 2016 presidential debates concluded that they actually strengthened polarization as those with the strongest partisan social identity, more confident in their views, tweeted less strong partisans, strengthening the bonds among a candidate's supporters (FJ 145).

So sensitive was the Trump campaign to the importance of this phenomenon that that prior to the second debate, Trump tweeted, "My team of deplorables will be taking over my Twitter account for tonight's #debate" (WH 70).

I don't want, however, to write off presidential debates completely. A debate in which each candidate was given six minutes for an opening statement and say four minutes for a close would at least allow the candidate to present himself in a controlled way that measured more than the ability to parry and thrust. Also, why not give candidates the questions in advance and make them public so voters could be debating the issues right along with the candidates. There also should be some opportunity for candidates to question each other. Several debates organized along these lines would in fact be educational and give voters a much better way of viewing the candidates. As I mention in Appendix V, Kennedy and Nixon each were given eight minutes for opening statements in their first debate.

Robust free speech assumes that people are amenable to persuasion. That assumption has been proven again and again to be a correct one.

When people learn the truth, they do change, they can overcome their fears. Take the people of Morristown, Tennessee who, as reported by NPR, woke up one morning to find helicopters flying overhead, the local meat-packing plant cordoned off, and scores of undocumented workers — many with families — under arrest. It made national news

Morristown is a close-knit community of roughly 30,000 people. Hispanics have lived there peacefully with their neighbors for years in the heart of the Biblebelt among a very conservative population that gave Trump 77% of its vote in 2016. But the raid stunned the community. In very short order, more than $90,000 was raised for bond money to help secure the release of the workers. These donors were people who had bought completely into the illusion, so assiduously cultivated by Trump, that deportations would be aimed at criminals and drug-dealers. Indeed, in his address at Gettysburg late in the campaign those were the people Trump promised to go after. These raids contradicted that promise. A rally was held a day or so after the raid in which many children pleaded for the return of their parent or parents. The emotional impact for many non-Hispanics in the community was devastating. This was not what they thought they had voted for.

These are people with fundamentally decent values, people who liberals might have thought they had very little in common with had they focused solely on their differing views on guns or abortion.

Other examples on a larger scale abound. In the fifties and sixties, gay men and women were completely hidden, aware that any revelation of their status would be devastating for their personal lives. Today, a significant majority of the country approves of gay marriage and even more agree that discrimination against gays is simply wrong. Slowly over time, the public at large recognized that the demonized were in fact their neighbors, friends, and their own family. In the area of race relations, it may have taken *Brown v. Board of Education*, the ugliness of Little Rock, the sit-ins, Freedom rides, Bull Connor, the Birmingham bombing, and Selma but suddenly what had been going on for more than half a century in the South was no longer acceptable. Reality could no longer be ignored.

The volunteerism so much a part of our daily life finds no more important an outlet than at election time. Private citizens still make up the infrastructure of our elections just as they did sixty years ago. Buttons and bumper stickers may not be prevalent any more but lawn signs seem to have come of age. In many rural communities Trump signs grew like wildflowers. On both sides, volunteers still poll watch, write letters to the newspaper, make phone calls, lick envelopes, canvas neighborhoods, register voters, man headquarters and take people to the polls. In the end, every four years, *We the People* still own this process. That fundamental dynamic has not changed though much else has.

The most basic requirement of any democratic society is that both sides accept the results of its elections. Now it seems that this assumption may be up for grabs. Republican legislators in no fewer than three states — Michigan, North Carolina, and Wisconsin — passed legislation after the 2018 election to limit the powers of a Governor who was soon to be not of their party. A Republican Governor and legislature in Florida have even tried to overrule their own voters, enacting legislation that significantly undermines the recently enacted constitutional amendment allowing felons who have served their time to vote. It must be said that the refusal from day one of many to accept the legitimacy of Trump's presidency — even trying to get Trump electors to change their votes — is also a species of this phenomenon.

These developments are deeply disturbing. Acceptance of election results is a predicate for any democracy. In 1800, Alexander Hamilton tried to persuade then New York Governor John Jay — both were Federalists — to reverse the method of choosing electors that the Federalist legislature had initially chosen after it became clear that the method would give all of the State's votes to Jefferson. Jay refused to sanction the scheme and New York provided Jefferson's margin of victory. The stakes couldn't have been higher; Jay's integrity elected as President a man he vehemently opposed.

In the coming years we will have to come to grips with all sorts of issues as the internet and mobile devices continue to create an entirely new social and economic universe. As automation and ever more powerful computers replace activities formerly performed by human beings, the very notion of what constitutes a meaningful daily life is called into question. And as we gain more control of our biological destiny and master the genome, the very notion of what it means to be a human being will also be in play.

Can our democracy work out these issues intelligently? The answer is yes — but only in an atmosphere of respect and civility where differing ideas can be constructively debated. The great danger, I believe, that Trump's re-election would pose in the long run, is not whatever short term damage he can do to our institutions — as I've indicated I think they are simply much too strong for him — but the impact four more years of his presidency would have on our ability to imagine we are all part of the same country.

4. Why Centrism is Essential and What It Means

Today, words like moderation, centrism, and compromise have very little cachet. Much better, it is thought, to be fully engaged, ready for battle, loyal to your cause. *Give me Liberty or Give me Death.* There is a reason summer camps love color wars. Conflict is inherently more exciting than the tedious task of negotiating reasonable solutions.

The return to some semblance of true bipartisanship where there is a genuine effort to resolve differences by means other than the force of a majority vote would be greatly assisted by a fundamentally different approach to politics on the part of both voters and their representatives.

That approach I will call "centrism." I mean it not as a midpoint in the political spectrum, not at all a 'let's split the difference at all costs' attitude. Rather, I see it as an attitude toward politics in general. Clearly, its hallmark is a willingness to consider all the possible ways to attack a problem without pre-conceived biases against one set of solutions because of their source.

A centrist, as I define the concept, can embrace non-middle-ground solutions. You can be a centrist and end up supporting Medicare for All as long as you have carefully considered all alternatives and genuinely seek to incorporate good ideas from the other side. It is how one arrives at one's conclusions that make one a centrist. It is an attitude that prizes an open mind on any given issue or problem. Yes, the sum total of one's positions will lead to defining one's overall political outlook in a way that will likely put one on one side or other of the political spectrum — the idea of a perfect midpoint is itself illusory — but it will be the product of actually thinking through one's views, in itself a kind of introspection that can actually be very enriching from a personal standpoint. In attempting to arrive at your own conclusions, you actually get to know yourself a little better.

An example. I am a strong believer in and advocate for gay rights. I believe that the U.S. Constitution does protect a right of same sex marriage. I also believe, however, that the First Amendment might also protect a baker from having personally to create a wedding cake for a same sex couple given a deep belief that same sex marriage is wrong. We prize freedom of conscience in our democracy. We allowed conscientious objectors to avoid military service during World War II and in subsequent conflicts even though it meant that someone else might die in the objector's place. It is a close question because discrimination against gays is also wrong. The point is not whatever view one ultimately arrives at but simply to be open to arguments on both sides and not feel that you owe it to some ideological team to come out a certain way.

In addition to open-mindedness, centrism also demands empathy because trying to understand both sides of an issue or problem forces you to stand in someone else's shoes. This was the point that Arlie Hochschild was making when she urged her University of California, Berkeley friends and her new Louisiana friends to recognize how each of their own views are molded by their experiences and circumstances.

I do not mean that we should all be centrists or that the more ideologically inclined have no place. Quite the contrary. Deeply committed conservatives and progressives serve an important purpose. They challenge our thinking and often are the source of our most creative ideas. They also tend to be the most passionate citizens in our democracy. a good thing if leavened by a willingness to listen and respect for other viewpoints.

Am I being too idealistic in defining centrism in these terms? The thought has occurred to me so I was delighted to read a piece in late July 2019 by Thomas Friedman in which he seemed to share my understanding of what centrism should be:

> ....I prefer not to call myself a "centrist." That statement implies someone whose views are mush, situated between two clearly defined polls of left and right. My views are not mush. *They just emerge from a different approach to politics.* (Friedman's emphasis though it would have been mine as well). (TF)

A distinguished conservative, Yuval Levin, even more explicitly than Friedman, made the case that all shades of opinion have a place if they simply try to hear each other. In a speech at the National Conservatism Conference in Washington D.C. in July 2019, he noted, "Those with whom we disagree in our society are not our enemies; they are our neighbors. They are not out to do harm to our country; they differ with us about what would be good for it." Then, he added:

> We should not allow ourselves to fall into the hysterical fear of the supposed advances and victories of these ideological adversar-

ies. They are a minority as we are. They are mostly failing too. And their task, no less than ours, is to persuade a larger society that is not so sure that either side of our politics has got its head on straight (ST).

The centrists should be that larger society, the mediators in the clash of the ideologues in which everyone has a role to play.

Moderation is different than the kind of centrism I am searching for; it does not quite make the same demands. Moderation is simply an impulse born of recognizing the desirability of fashioning compromises that will engender the largest amount of public support for legislation. In other words, a moderate is someone who moderates his own views, no matter how arrived at, in the interest of seeing results. When one party completely controls both Congress and the presidency, moderation may seem less important but even then, given the filibuster rule in the U.S. Senate, moderation is often still the only road to accomplishment. Moderation does assume that many problems and issues are amenable to compromise.

The great virtue of solutions that attract at least some level of support from the other side is their permanence.

Though the final structure of the bill establishing Medicare and Medicaid was much more Democratic in its orientation, the bill itself was the result of many hearings and much debate and, in the end, attracted the support of more than one-half of the House Republicans and thirteen out of thirty Republicans in the Senate. The Voting Rights Act of 1965 passed with overwhelming bipartisan support in both houses of Congress (82% of Republicans supported it in the House). In 1972, a bipartisan coalition overrode the veto of President Nixon of the Clean Water Act who had objected to its price tag. The equally iconic Clean Air Act passed the Senate in 1970 without a single negative vote and under the first President Bush it was strengthened by a vote of 89-11. The comprehensive Tax Reform Act of 1986 was a product of intense debate and compromises leading ultimately to its enactment by a majority of both parties in the House and a vote of 74 to 23 in the Senate. Twice during the Reagan administration Congress enacted and Reagan signed civil rights legislation effectively overturning Supreme Court decisions narrowly construing provisions of the Civil Rights laws and then again in 1991, President Bush did the same. All three acts enjoyed bipartisan support although in 1990 President Bush vetoed an earlier form of the Civil Rights Act of 1991. Compromises were made and the legislation subsequently passed.

Moderation makes no demand that one surrender one's principles. And at any given point, one party has a majority and will obviously have the upper hand in any conversation, but moderation is an instinct that understands that broad based solutions, as long as the majority's basic objective is not compromised, are always preferable.

There are, of course, some differences that are so emotionally laden that exchanges of views seem almost beside the point.

Abortion is certainly one example but in a sense it is the exception that proves the rule. Though I believe that the Constitution does protect a woman's right to choose, even Justice Ginsburg felt that *Roe v. Wade* should have been decided in a way that still allowed for political discussions and the possibility of meaningful legislative solutions. By taking the issue out of state legislative hands altogether, the Court gave no chance for the two sides to constructively explore possible compromises or at least hear each other out. Instead we have had a forty-five year war with one side doing everything to reverse the decision and undermine its intent and the other understandably fighting to preserve it.

The result is a pro-life movement that sought and finally found an Alabama legislature willing to enact legislation that completely eliminates choice, even in the case of rape or incest, and threatens doctors who perform abortion with 99 years in prison. The movement has also succeeded in winning severe restrictions in other states, including laws outlawing abortions after a fetal heart-beat has been detected — sometimes a point at which a woman does not even know she is pregnant. A dialogue rather than a war might have also led to a concession by the pro-choice side that some reasonable burdens on the exercise of choice could provide a politically acceptable compromise in states where the overwhelming majority disapproved of abortion.

We have paid a steep price for our new polarization. When career politicians judge every question from the standpoint of their own interest and see more danger in agreeing than in disagreeing, we all suffer. Huge problems — immigration, the deficit, student debt, climate change, gun control, child care, long-term joblessness and health care — fester and grow worse. Tens of millions of lives are now affected by these issues. It makes 2020 the most important election of this century, a subject to which we now turn.

Chapter 4
Looking to November 3, 2020

Recall that in 2016, 25% of those who voted for Donald Trump thought he was temperamentally unfit to be the President of the United States. Around 51% of all voters thought that Hillary Clinton had the right temperament to be president. Yet Trump won. Unfathomable? Not really. Of the millions of voters who had made change their main priority, more than three-fourths voted for Donald Trump.

So two questions immediately loom for Trump voters in 2020: first, did Trump deliver the change they wanted? This is a particularly salient question for the many in the crowds at Trump rallies for whom, Jenna Johnson, recalled, "there's an overwhelming feeling that the economy is still not doing well enough – and a resignation that it might never get any better than this without some dramatic change" (JJ). A second question of particular importance for more traditional Republicans, particularly moderates and more affluent conservatives disturbed by many aspects of Trump's behavior, is simply "was it worth it" and, even if it was, is it time to say "no more?"

As of August 2019, at least twenty candidates are actively seeking the Democratic nomination. It is impossible to predict who will win but prognostication is not the purpose of this chapter. As Yogi Berra may have said, "it is difficult to make predictions, especially about the future." But clearly, there is a great deal of optimism among Democrats surrounding the 2020 election.

Even, however, with the well-earned reservations about him personally, beating Trump will be an enormous challenge. The President controls the news cycle because everything he does or says is by virtue of his office important. He can also manipulate events in his favor, for example, coming to an agreement with China on trade that will allow him to claim victory even if it achieves very little of what he originally sought. Trump will also not be outspent in the coming campaign as he was, two one, by Hillary in 2016. History is also on his side. The last three Presidents have all won re-election.

His greatest asset may be the economy although, as of August 2019, there are warning signs of a possible coming recession. Today, the unemployment rate stands at a fifty-year low, 3.7%. Moreover, the jury is still out on a number of his more controversial decisions. His aggressive sanctions against Iran after withdrawing from the nuclear deal might conceivably force Iran to make a more favorable agreement given the toll they are taking on the Iranian economy. How his Korean initiative will end is not known. Another huge factor in his favor will be that he has delivered a major part of the Republican agenda: huge tax reductions, deregulation and two conservative Supreme Court justices. More Supreme Court vacancies may beckon — an important incentive for many of his supporters in 2016. He will surely have a united party behind him, something that is not a given for the Democrats at this point after four bruising primary debates.

And then there is love of the fight for its own sake. Whether carefully calculated or borne of racial animus – it could be both – his attacks on four newly elected women of color in the House of Representatives Party keeps the news cycle focused exactly where Trump wants it: on the far left of the Democratic Party. It also subliminally reminds white voters just which party is home to the people who look least like them.

Politics can make strange bedfellows, none stranger than the coalition of northern liberals and arch segregationists that kept the Democrats in power for twenty years between 1932 and 1952. All the focus on Trump's personality should not obscure a Republican coalition of, in the words of Nolan McCarty et al., the "affluent, the 'moral', and working-class whites" (NM 236).

A key question for the Democrats is whether they can make inroads, even small ones, into this coalition. If the contest in the rustbelt states is close, making those small inroads could well spell the difference between victory and defeat. It is why every vote counts.

At this juncture, the news for the Democrats is not altogether good. In the first set of Democratic debates, many candidates took positions for decriminalizing illegal border entry, providing Medicaid to undocumented immigrants and ending all private insurance through Medicare For All. It did not go unnoticed. A subsequent New York Times article found that many of Trump's Michigan voters were staying with him. One Republican strategist noted that even Republicans who didn't vote for Trump the first time are considering voting for him now "given where Democrats are landing on policy," something that is "really frightening people" (SS-NYT)

Both parties will be facing defining moments in the near future but the Democrats' will come first in 2020 as they struggle to choose a nominee who can appeal to independents and moderates while igniting real enthusiasm among their base. (The Republican defining moment will happen in 2024 when the party will need to decide whether to stay in Oz without the Wizard or somehow get back to Kansas.)

In Chapter 3 I tried to make the case for civility and openness to ideas from all sides and argued that our constitutional system of checks and balances cannot function effectively in the absence of such spirit. But when it comes to elections, we are in different waters, for this is the time when parties should delineate their differences and advance their ideas clearly and boldly. Only then can an election stand for something.

I would very much like to have a new President inaugurated in January 2021 and believe there are important things for the Democratic Party to both do and avoid if that is to happen. I think Trump would be pleased to know, as I indicated in Chapter 2, that I thought he ran the superior campaign in 2016. I do not, however, want to see the President re-elected. Most of this chapter will offer unsolicited advice aimed at avoiding that result

First, however, since Trump now has a primary opponent of his own in the person of William Weld, I begin with a brief consideration of that challenge. Weld was Gary Johnson's running mate in 2016 on the Libertarian ticket. He is an interesting combination. He is strongly pro-choice and pro-gay rights. In fact, as Governor of Massachusetts, he helped encourage the first gay-straight alliances in public schools. He is also, however, a strong fiscal conservative very intent on balancing the federal budget and a believer in charter schools.

Though Weld's views on abortion make him an outlier in today's Republican Party, it still will be interesting to see what level of support he achieves, particularly in the swing states. Most observers see a Weld candidacy as weakening Trump for the general election. That might not be the case if Trump were a different person, one who might respond to the challenge by reaching out to those least enamored of him within the Republican Party and independents as well. Any such generosity on Trump's part would, of course, raise suspicion of a stunt double. Still, a primary will give him a great excuse to hold the kinds of campaign type rallies he loves and for strategists to try out campaign themes.

Republican success since 1980 has been predicated on the ability of the party to unify two kinds of voters: those concerned mainly with social issues like abortion, gun rights and freedom for religious conscience, and traditional business-oriented Republicans concerned more with issues like deregulation, free trade and lower taxes. These two wings of the Republican Party haven't really needed to agree with each other since they are simply interested in different things. In this respect, very little has changed. Trump's success in 2016 was in adding to this mix a new element, namely voters who had never really been moved to participate in electoral politics at all for the simple reason that until Trump, they detested all politicians.

Given the advantage of incumbency and likely a good economy, why do so many Democrats want to win the privilege of challenging Trump? I think it is only partly due to his personal unpopularity and the feeling that we have a President whose word cannot ever be trusted. Buoyed by the results of 2018, there is also a justifiable feeling that his has turned out to be a far-right administration fundamentally out of sync with the views of a majority of the country.

The tax cuts, for example, did not win the widespread approval Republicans had hoped for. The reasons are not hard to discern. Although the nonpartisan Tax Policy Center estimated that up to 80% of Americans would see some reduction in their federal taxes, it was very small for most, particularly in comparison to the tax cuts that corporations and wealthy individuals received. The Tax Policy Center has projected that roughly three-fifths of lower income taxpayers will have federal tax savings of less than $1,000 compared to $51,000 for the top 1% (TG). Also, it appears indisputable that the biggest beneficiaries of the tax bill were corporations, their basic rate dropping from 35% to 21%. Interestingly, the corporate cut is permanent while the individual rate cuts expire after 2025.

The impact of the tax cuts on the deficit would have caused the pre-Trump Republican Party grave concern. Though the Congressional Budget Office has estimated that deficits will average 4.4% of GDP between now and 2029, much higher than the average 2.9% from the previous fifty years, the G.O.P. seems perfectly happy with its handiwork.

In announcing his candidacy in 2016, Trump had declared that if the national debt reached $24 trillion (it was roughly $20 trillion when he took office) "we become Greece, That's when we become a country that is unsalvageable." Given the effect of the Republican tax legislation, it seems likely that we will reach $24 trillion by the end of his term and, by Trump's own description our economy will become "unsalvageable." The total federal debt — growing every year with the deficits — will reach an estimated 93% of GDP by 2029 (TG).

To some extent, the road map for the Democratic Party in 2020 had a dry run in 2018 and did very well. The results of that election and the reasons for Democratic success are not hard to discern. A key was that Independents broke for Democrats by a 12-point margin (WG). In the prior midterm election of 2014, independents went for the Republicans by exactly the same margin. Republicans lost support in both the suburbs and rural areas (WG). Democrats talked primarily about health care and avoided talk of impeachment. In the election both party's bases remained loyal, 94% of Republicans voting for their candidate and 95% of Democrats doing the same. For one important Republican consultant group, "the most important takeaway from this data is that neither party's base is large enough to produce a winning majority" (WG).

There were other important findings. New voters almost certainly helped Democrats retake the House. According to CBS News exit polling, 17% of those who turned out in the midterms were new voters. It is hard to imagine them voting in 2018 and not in 2020. In the 2010 midterms in which Republicans stormed back into the majority, just 3% were new voters. College educated white women did what the Clinton campaign hoped for in 2016, increasing their support for Democrats by 8 percentage points.

Another reason for optimism for Democrats: Hillary Clinton won 58 percent of voters between the ages of voters 18 to 29. Each progression in age gave Trump increasing levels of support. He won voters age 65 and over by a margin of 55 percent to 45 percent. Consequently, if the voters of 2016 maintain their current loyalties as they age up, the Democrats will likely benefit in 2020 demographically as they receive a fresh infusion of new voters and an increasing share of the progressively aging vote. A recent Pew survey shows that 57% of millennials describe themselves as liberal, only 12% conservative, a fact with huge long-term implications beyond 2020.

Millennials are not likely to change their outlook anytime soon. Indeed, the Pew Research Center Study also has found that 23% of its 18 to 29 year-old respondents who identified as Republican in December 2015 had left the party in March 2017; only 9% of Democrats had defected. (ED 162).

So there is every reason to believe that Democrats have a good chance to win if they talk about things people care about, find an appealing candidate, and present a unified front where both the progressive and more centrist elements of the party are fully behind their nominee.

A central strategic question is how vigorously the party needs to reach beyond itself to Independents and winnable Republicans. One observer, Paul Waldman, has written that "the entire electability discussion assumes that if there are lots of sexist voters and lots of racist voters, then they must be courted and flattered and catered to, lest they become too angry and vote for Trump." Waldman then adds "the idea that the path to success for a Democrat might lie elsewhere — say, with the candidate best able to organize and mobilize the millions of African-Americans and Latinos who would vote Democratic if they went to the polls — never enters the electability discussion. We seem unable to consider the ability to mobilize votes as a factor in electability, despite all the copious evidence that it is" (PW). Waldman is partly right. No Democrat will win without a strong turnout from the party's base. But both 2016 and 2018 testify to the fact that turning out your base is not enough. You must have a message that appeals to a broad swath of voters. African-American turnout was less for Clinton than it was for Obama, something that had to be expected. Trump won, however, because he persuaded millions of Obama supporters to support his candidacy, winning or almost winning historic Democratic bastions like Luzerne and Erie Counties in Pennsylvania.

Donald Trump did not create our polarization, but he has exploited it to an almost unimaginable extent. He may or not be racist in his heart but it doesn't really matter. The sum total of his behavior recently led conservative radio talk show host and former Congressman (elected with Tea Party support) Joe Walsh to plead for a primary challenge to Trump from the Republican Right.

Unlike the criminal law, in politics intent is irrelevant. It's the impact of one's words and the message they convey that is crucial, in no case more significantly than when uttered by the President of the United States. So when a President goes out of his way to single out four Congresswomen of color for unrelenting condemnation, seeks to inflame the country against a Black professional football player for expressing his disapproval of racial injustice, seems to equate white supremacists and their protesters, constantly harps on the crimes of undocumented immigrants even though their crime rate is lower than that for the population at large, talks about an Hispanic "invasion," and portrays black areas of our cities as hell holes with all the subliminal messages about African Americans those oversimplified, inaccurate descriptions convey, it is not surprising why white supremacists, whether rightly or wrongly, feel they have a kindred spirit in the White House.

It is more than about race. We have a president who continuously says things that are demonstrably untrue and who feels free to insinuate the worst about everyone. He characterizes as fake news any reporting, no matter how accurate, that he doesn't like. Russian interference in the 2016 election is only the most glaring example. He feels comfortable using the word "treason" about his Democratic opponents. At one of his rallies, he accused Democrats of favoring infanticide. He loves to imply the worst about anybody if it suits his purposes: he once said about President Obama: "We're being led by a man who is either not tough, not smart, or else he's got something else in mind. He can't even mention the words 'radical Islamic terrorism. *There's something going on* (my emphasis)." In April 2019, speaking to the National Rifle Association, Trump asserted that the Mueller investigation was nothing less than an attempted "coup," one, fortunately, he added, he was able to defeat without guns.

Almost every day, the President says something that could be added to this litany.

And then there is what amounts to a frontal attack on science itself. Four more years of a President who refused to sign a communiqué on protecting the warming artic region unless it was stripped of all reference to climate change and who regards the Environmental Protection Agency as part of the "deep state" is simply four years too many.

It is hard to think of a president or leader less evocative of Hemingway's phrase "grace under pressure" than Trump, a man who constantly reminds us what a genius he is and accepts no responsibility for anything that goes wrong, a man who lauds the leader of the most totalitarian regime on the planet while stereotyping an entire population by its worst elements. There is a reason why a number of national champion sports teams no longer choose to celebrate their accomplishments at the White House.

There is a chasm between what Trump promised and what has happened. He said our infrastructure was a disgrace but has produced nothing to address it. He said he would bring down the deficit but his tax legislation has ballooned it. He was going to repeal Obamacare and replace it with something much better with lower premiums and greater coverage; all he has done instead is wage guerilla war against it while causing real harm to his own supporters. His peerless negotiating skills, he said, would cause Mexico to pay for a wall across our southern border. Instead, he had to ask Congress for the money and declared what is likely an unconstitutional state of emergency when he didn't get it. He promised to reduce illegal southern border crossings and instead cut off funds to the very Central American countries whose internal violence was creating these mass migrations in the first place. He promised to focus deportation efforts on dangerous criminals and instead threatens mass deportations. After the massacre in Parkland, Florida, he first embraced a proposal for universal background checks. The next day the NRA came calling and Trump quickly reversed himself. He expressed his compassion for Dreamers and then removed their administrative protection. He promised a huge tax cut for the middle class and instead delivered one for our most powerful corporations. He has joked with President Putin about Russian interference with our election and valued Putin's denials over the findings of his own intelligence agencies. He gives comfort to European leaders intent on creating pseudo democracies and undermines the leaders of real ones. And now his trade war with China and tariff policies elsewhere may be contributing to the onset of a global recession.

This is by no means a complete catalog of the shortcomings of the Trump administration or the many ways it has hurt the country, but is enough, I hope, to show that the stakes are very high in the coming election, both for the long and short term. How should the Democrats respond?

Recent history, I think, provides an important clue. The last two Democrats who won the Presidency — Barack Obama and Bill Clinton — shared one thing: personal appeal based on an ability to articulate their message clearly and convincingly. Call it charisma if you like but it was a quality that made people want to listen to them. People liked being in their presence, meaning for most, in their living rooms. None of the last four Democrats to lose their presidential races had this quality. They would all have made, in my judgment, good Presidents. But neither Mike Dukakis, Al Gore, John Kerry, nor Hillary Clinton gained traction from their public personas. Perhaps even the reverse. Recall Mike Dukakis's professorial response to a debate question about how he would feel about capital punishment if his wife was raped, Al Gore's constant sighing in the first debate, John Kerry's allowing himself to be swift-boated during the summer of 2004, and Hillary's belief that it would be impossible to alter a largely negative view of who she was.

If the studies are correct that roughly 75% to 80% of voters do not follow politics closely and often are willing to align their own views to fit the candidate's, then clearly personal appeal becomes an enormously important attribute. The first question Democratic primary voters might wisely ask themselves is not which candidate echoes most closely their own beliefs but which candidate has personal qualities that will enable him or her to connect most effectively with the American people and particularly those independents and moderates most likely to decide the election. This is not to say that a candidate's positions are unimportant, simply that they are not the threshold question. If elections were decided on the basis of thoughtful policy responses, Hillary Clinton would have won in a landslide. More is required.

Given the kind of person the President has proven himself to be and how he has chosen to govern, a Democratic candidate who gives some assurance of a more normal presidency would certainly provide what many voters might perceive as a refreshing change.

As already alluded to, no Democratic candidate will be able to win if all elements of the Democratic Party are not solidly behind him or her. That will not be an easy task, whomever the nominee might be, for the Democrats do embrace a wide range of viewpoints and policy prescriptions. Some embrace free tuition at public colleges, Medicare for All, a wealth tax, a government program of universal child-care and complete elimination of fossil fuel use within two decades or less. For others, these goals are unrealistic, unwise and or a recipe for electoral disaster.

The good news, however, is that even the Democrats for whom the more far-reaching proposals are a bridge too far share a set of common values with most of the brethren to their left. Almost all Democrats regard health care as a right not a privilege, want to make college more affordable, lessen the burden of student debt, advance women's rights, give strong support for working mothers with children, and address problems of institutional racism, income inequality, mass shootings and climate change. They also share in the desire for progressive Supreme Court justices.

The Democrats forget that commonality at their peril.

I myself, a strong believer in the private sector, would clearly be placed in the moderate, perhaps even conservative spectrum of Democratic politics. Still, I feel myself fully committed to the fundamental outlook of the Democratic Party. In a recent column in The Wall Street Journal, Andy Kessler, extolling the virtues of capitalism, condemned as modern-day Luddites those workers who sometimes seek to protect their jobs in the face of automation. Kessler singled out a provision in the postal union workers contract that required existing workers to be offered any new jobs created by automation. This, Kessler went on, is "one reason, even with automation, we still have 500,000 postal workers when the right number is zero" (AK). How airily Kessler dismisses the notion that there might be anything to concern us with half a million workers suddenly without employment. The fact is that efficiency is not the highest virtue and capitalism is a failure unless it produces a widely shared prosperity and encourages communities full of engaged and personally meaningful lives.

We are now more than three decades into a period when the successes of American and global capitalism have come at an ever-increasing cost, for the singular fact of this period is how corporate profits have come at the expense of Corporate America's own workers, leading to a huge loss of manufacturing jobs and a decline in median income while the most affluent get richer and richer. In a world of global competition and rapid automation, companies seek every edge, including moving to cheap labor markets abroad and sheltering profits there as well. They don't do it because they're inherently evil; they do it to survive and because profits, dividends and capital gains are the name of the game. But the consequences for many in this country have been deadly.

People feel less secure for a reason; they are less secure. The number of employer-sponsored defined benefit plans has declined precipitously since the dawn of the Reagan era. Today, approximately half of all workers do not have access to any employer-sponsored retirement plan at all.

Democrats in the coming days need to advance an agenda and ideas that emphasize both a comfort with the private sector and an intelligent case for correcting the imbalances it has created. There is room for a healthy debate within the Democratic Party over the whole gamut of ideas that have been floated on various key issues but I think we imperil our chances when we seem to be demonizing any element of the population, even the 1%. There is much, for example, that I admire about Senator Elizabeth Warren. She fought hard against deeply unfair changes to the bankruptcy laws and championed the national Consumer Financial Protection Board that many Republicans would like to eliminate altogether, including President Trump. But I cringe when she rails against the 1% as if they are bloodsuckers when in fact many are enormously wealthy because the capitalist system rewards entrepreneurial success in extravagant ways. By and large, appealing to a kind of class-consciousness has rarely been a recipe for success in American politics and there is no indication that it will be any more successful now.

In a recent piece in *The New York Times*, Jonathan Alter argued that many of today's progressive proposals, such as universal Pre-K, baby bonds, and Medicare for All, are animated by the same spirit that characterized FDR's New Deal, namely to "reform capitalism so that it worked better for ordinary people" (JA). He pointed out, however, two other things as well: first, that FDR had the "advantage" of advancing his agenda for a nation mired in Depression and willing to embrace virtually any program that offered some hope for a change, and second, that Roosevelt was no socialist but a pragmatist who could reject measures he thought too extreme, like nationalizing the banks. Alter clearly admires many parts of Elizabeth Warren's agenda but he warns that "today's economic anxieties might not be powerful enough to drive real change." I'm not sure what Alter meant by real change and would disagree to the extent he thinks that a public option, for example, for health insurance does not constitute real change. But his larger message is important. We are not in desperate economic times. Though the economy doesn't work well enough for enough people, few would deny its underlying strength.

Donald Trump will make every effort to demonize the Democratic Party and scare the electorate into believing that the choice in 2020 will be between him and the private enterprise system on the one hand and the Democrats and socialism on the other. If he succeeds in making that case, he will win. Democrats will make Trump's case for him if they present their program as a means to radically restructure a dystopian economy. If, on the other hand, the Democrats offer their economic program in the spirit of optimism, pragmatism and problem solving, they will make Trump's task exceedingly difficult.

Trump will cry socialism at whatever programs Democrats suggest and the fact is that many in the Democratic Party, particularly young people, do not shrink from that term. What passes for socialism today, however, is not the classic socialism of an earlier time when it was much more closely associated with government ownership of the means of production and a heavily planned economy. Today, it is part of the Republican mantra to sweep any progressive programs aimed at helping even the broad middle class as "socialistic." Democrats must be ready to counter that red herring by reminding voters that virtually every major widely accepted program aimed at benefitting the broad swath of ordinary citizens – social security, Medicare, Medicaid, food stamps -- was initially decried by their opponents as creeping socialism.

The need for a more inclusive capitalism, one sensitive to society's broader needs and problems including the environment, seems to be gaining recognition even in the business community. In late August 2019, the Business Roundtable, comprised of 200 leading corporate executives including the heads of JP Morgan, Amazon and General Motors, issued a report urging corporations to recognize workers and the community at large as important stakeholders to whom corporations owed a clear responsibility. Whether this is just appealing rhetoric or a real sea change in corporate outlook, of course, remains to be seen. But it is, I think, recognition of the need to address some of our deeper problems.

"Socialism" will not be Trump's only line of attack. For the conspiracy-minded, he will continue to rail against the deep state, and for social conservatives he will portray America as engaged, to use the words of Newt Gingrich, in a "cultural-political war — a fight over our very identity as a people." In his recent book, Gingrich reveals the kind of attack the Democratic nominee might expect:

On one side of this conflict is a factional anti-Trump coalition – a strange amalgam of radicals, liberals, globalists, establishment elites from both parties, and blatantly anti-American groups loosely held together by their hostility to and disdain for the President. On the other side is Trump's America — the millions of hardworking people who are united by respect for our foundational freedoms, traditional values, and history of limited commonsense government (NG 3).

These are large themes. They need to be opposed with a counter narrative, another story if you will, that focuses on the many ways in which Trump is essentially a phony populist whose policies betray "the millions of hardworking Americans" whom Gingrich claims for "Trump's America." But even more importantly, Democrats must explain why their proposals are more in line with "fundamental freedoms" than Republican ones, why they better reflect our "true values as a people" and why Democrats believe in a "commonsense government" that includes sensible regulation to make sure that our strong entrepreneurial private enterprise system works for everybody but not regulation that strangles our spirit of free enterprise.

But it isn't just about economics and material things. The Party must confront the country with a fundamental question: Even if you are not fully in line with Democratic proposals and maybe have never voted Democratic in your life, does Trump truly represent the kinds of values that have made America great, or does he, in fact, represent the exact opposite? This must be an argument not just about Trump but as importantly – actually more importantly – who we think we are as a people.

Shortly after the 2018 election, Sabrina Tavernise reported on a "deep study" of the electorate undertaken by the non-partisan organization, More In Common. The study found that more than two-thirds of the 8,000 voters it interviewed, comprised a group it called the Exhausted Majority. More than one-third did not vote in 2016. The project resulted in a 190-page report entitled "Hidden Tribes." Tavernise summarized the report this way:

> The study shows that most Americans have political tastes that are not uniform: They may lean toward one party, but they see things they like in both. Its findings suggest a deep hunger for political leaders who are practical and not tribal — who do not cast the world in starkly moral terms but in bread and butter policy terms.
>
> The approval of several ballot initiatives long supported by Democrats but opposed by Republicans in Republican or Republican-leaning States last week might have signaled the power of the Exhausted Majority to break partisan gridlock. Those included a measure in Florida that re-enfranchised former felons; measures in Idaho, Nebraska and Utah that expanded Medicaid; and minimum wage measures in Arkansas and Missouri. (ST).

The ballot initiatives the report references are important. They suggest that when voters are focused on specific issues with a liberal/conservative dimension they will embrace liberal positions even in conservative states.

But other results are also instructive. For example, Colorado, a swing state that went for Clinton, simultaneously rejected by more than a 3 to 1 margin an amendment to the Colorado Constitution which would have guaranteed healthcare for all Colorado residents, to be paid for by a 10% payroll tax. Approval ratings for Medicare for All plummet when voters are advised of the potential cost and how it would affect their own health care. While Bernie Sanders makes a strong case for overhauling health care, many of the objections raised to his plan — initial cost, painful transition, elimination of an entire industry (health insurance) with attendant unemployment and the general happiness of many with their current insurance — almost certainly would resonate strongly to the Democrats' detriment in the general election.

Race, immigration, climate change and healthcare are hugely important issues. Democrats, however, should not overlook less discussed areas amenable to the kind of pragmatic approaches that can be addressed with targeted solutions. This is not just a recipe for governance but would be very helpful politically, for the more specific the problem, the more likely it is to affect a discrete set of voters.

Let me provide a few examples.

A recent article in *The New York Times* described the coming tsunami for seniors when, within a decade, most won't be able to afford assisted living (PS). Even modest proposals in the direction of addressing this concern would grab the attention of the group (over 65) from which Trump grew his strongest support.

Men and women who lose their jobs in their fifties and even forties face huge hurdles fighting age discrimination in trying to regain employment. Recent opinions of two federal circuit courts of appeals make it harder for this group to sue under the federal statute outlawing age discrimination. A proposal for a legislative fix, as occurred with conservative federal civil rights decisions in the eighties, would not go unnoticed by this group.

One thing that unites both rural and urban America is that both are afflicted with communities desperately in need of help. A set of programs specifically focused on increasing private investment in both sets of communities would be one way of bridging the red/blue divide, a divide that occurs not only between states but within states as well. These programs could easily work through public/private initiatives, making them attractive to a broad spectrum of opinion.

National service is an idea that even many conservatives embrace. Hillary Clinton, as mentioned earlier, made it the focus of a major address; Donald Trump has proposed slashing the limited programs that already exist. Such programs, if given sufficient support, could be another targeted way of bringing improvements to depressed rural and urban areas. They would also help with unemployment and even increase rates of labor participation.

One of the main obstacles to a federal minimum wage is the very great difference in cost of living in different sections of the country and different kinds of areas. There is now, however, something called the Living Wage Calculator, first developed by Amy Glasmeier — that breaks down cost of living data county by county throughout the country. Why not a nuanced federal minimum wage proposal taking advantage of this tool. Also, some conservatives, sensitive to the growing disparities in wealth, have embraced increases in the earned income tax credit as a way of addressing this problem without the job loss that a minimum wage might entail. (Economists debate how great the job loss would be but few deny that there would be some.) There is no reason why Democrats can't offer some combination of these proposals.

Here's another problem. Between 2011 and 2017, the country lost four million low rent apartments; in many affluent cities, large numbers of people pay more than 50%

of their income for housing; homelessness is once again on the rise (LC). Yet, Liza Cohen, an American History Professor at Harvard, has noted that, except for a few Democratic hopefuls, "the political conversation around housing has been muted" (LC). Actually, 'non-existent' in any meaningful way would be closer to the truth. To meet the problem, Cohen suggests reinvigorated programs of mortgage subsidies to non-profits and private developers for constructing subsidized housing, expanded rent subsidies for tenants, and funding for housing for the elderly. It isn't just the elderly who suffer with the current situation. Many young people are living with their parents, not out of choice, but as the only way to accumulate savings for themselves rather than handing them over to a landlord.

There is one national crisis Democrats rarely talk about: on average twenty veterans a day commit suicide. It is a problem easily ignored since only a little over 1% of Americans have served in the war zones of Iraq and Afghanistan. As one veteran has said, "We go to war with our brothers but we're left to fight demons by ourselves." This is one of the few areas of the budget where Trump has sought substantial increases. That doesn't mean, however, that the Democrats must cede this problem to him. Rather, the Democrats, as a party, should commit itself to the project of cutting that rate significantly within the next five years and should devote itself to putting staff resources in Congress into proposing programs for that purpose. The Democrats should make it an issue of national priority because it is the right thing to do. It may also be good politics. Donald Trump received the vote of two-thirds of our veterans. There is no reason that has to be a permanent state of affairs.

The problems laid out above might seem like wonkish ideas but they are wonkish ideas with large potential beneficiaries. They are not bribes. They are ways of dealing with the problems created often in one way or another by the profound redistribution of wealth toward the very richest Americans that has marked our recent history.

The numbers are staggering. According to the Federal Reserve Board, household wealth increased by $20 trillion over the last decade. An incredible $16.1 trillion of that amount, 80%, went to the top 1%; the bottom 50% of the country received 2% of the gain. As for middle class Americans, a homeownership rate of 70% in 2004 had dropped to 60% by 2016. Other compelling statistics could be cited as well.

The kinds of problems and possible solutions discussed above are ones that any nominee, whether named Sanders or Biden or Warren or anyone else, can run on. There are others as well from embracing a public option for healthcare to advancing environmental goals like increasing research on climate change, re-establishing Obama environmental regulations, ending oil drilling on federal lands, rejoining the climate change accord, and committing to a meaningful jobs program to accompany green initiatives and protecting benefits of workers hurt by the transition away from fossil fuels.

Even where the Democrats appear at their most divided, there are opportunities for cooperation that will allow a unified front. There is nothing, for example, more important to Democratic prospects than a strong turnout of young voters and perhaps the most important issue for them is addressing the issue of climate change. Many are deeply committed to the idea of the "Green New Deal." Yet, as Harold Meyerson describes in a recent article in The American *Prospect*, "It didn't take long for a backlash against the Green New Deal to form" as unions feared for job losses in the mining, extractive and construction industries. There are, Meyerson points out, "close to one million workers, more or less, who could lose their jobs — many of them well paying — in a fossil-fuel free economy" (HM). Meyerson, however, also describes how decades earlier Phil Burton, California's legendary Democratic Congressman, successfully overcame the objections of workers in the lumber industry to his plan for expanding Redwood Park, California by providing for robust protection of benefits for workers losing their jobs as a result of the expansion. Burton's political solution suggests how a robust Green New Deal could be combined with an emphasis on job creation in the new energy industry and protection for workers in the old one, forging a real alliance among two distinct constituencies and age groups.

If come election time, the Democrats stand in the public mind for intelligent public policy, they will likely win not only the Presidency but possibly the Senate as well. If, on the other hand, they seem scattered, extreme and so pre-occupied with demonizing Trump they have nothing else to offer, then they will likely lose.

There are I think three great dangers for the Democratic Party and its candidate.

First, Trump, just as he did with Clinton, will assert that Democrats are for completely open borders with no regard for its economic consequences or its unfairness to those trying to enter the country legally. The Democrats need to combat this assertion. This does not mean that that Democrats should not talk about immigration. Roughly two-thirds of Americans support DACA, the policy that would protect undocumented persons brought here as children. But Democrats must also make clear that they believe in border security and put forth sensible steps to prevent illegal crossings. The plight of those fleeing to our borders requires compassion and begs for a more liberal asylum policy, allowing more refugees. But there

194 | WALTER FRANK

is no point in having a legal immigration policy at all if we do not take seriously the need to enforce our borders.

There are some today who sincerely believe in a globalized world in which the nation state has little place. Certainly, nationalism that is based on notions of racial or ethnic superiority is completely unacceptable. But a sincere patriotism does not have to spring from these motivations and this is particularly true of a nation whose entire history is a tribute to welcoming ethnic diversity. Most Americans, even those whose ancestors came chained on slave ships, take a justifiable pride in many aspects of the country's history. They also believe, rightly, that open borders are inconsistent with both nationhood and the rule of law.

At the same time, of course, we should – whenever Trump rants against chain migration – remind voters of immigrants like Wilmot Collins who came here as the husband of Maddie Collins and became the first black mayor of Helena, Montana. Our very identity is founded on being a symbol of hope and freedom for the entire world. There is nothing wrong in pointing out all the ways in which Trump tarnishes that symbol.

The second danger is purely internal. If Democratic voters stay home because they did not get their first choice of nominee, Donald Trump will be re-elected. Those running for the nomination can minimize that possibility by avoiding personal attacks on each other, even when exploring policy differences. In 1980 Ronald Reagan pledged never to speak ill of a fellow Republican when he was fighting to get the nomination. He kept his word and the result was that he emerged from the Republican Convention with a united, enthusiastic party behind him. When he chose his main rival, George H.W. Bush, to become his running mate, there was not a single word he had to take back. Gerald Ford, from whom Reagan had tried to wrest the Republican nomination in 1976 in a divisive contest, also enthusiastically supported and worked for him in the general election.

By way of contrast, Bernie Sanders, as previously recounted, did strongly imply that Hillary was a tool of Wall Street and could not really therefore be relied upon to work for a progressive agenda. Though he worked hard for her later, the damage was already done. The bottom line is that if the Democrats contending for the nomination keep their fire on Donald Trump and develop their own positive ideas, they will enhance their chances in November. But if they turn their fire on each other, particularly with personal attacks, they might well be paving the way for Trump's re-election.

There is one more trap the Democratic Party and its candidate need to avoid, for Republicans like to portray the Democratic Party as nothing more than a collection of interest groups: feminists, minorities, the young and the poor to whom it must cater to survive, a party with no larger vision that seeks only to redistribute wealth, not to create it.

In early April 2019, Peggy Noonan urged Joe Biden not to run for President, not because he had changed but because the Democratic Party had changed. The new Democratic Party, she wrote, is "more pinched, more abstractly aggrieved, more theoretical, less human. Now there's a mood not of *Everyone Can Rise but of Some Must Be Taken Down*" (PN). I do not believe that her description correctly describes the Democratic Party but it is undoubtedly how the opposition in different ways will try to portray it. We do need to make clear our deep commitment to minority rights and to addressing issues like mass incarceration and police brutality but we need to do it in a way that evokes broad principles that Americans can recognize as their own: fairness, justice, due process. If it's just a checklist, it's both patronizing and ineffective.

And, quite apart from the perception, it will not work for voters have many identities. The evangelical may also be a union officer, the gun rights advocate in need of an affordable health policy, the pro-life mother also somebody with a lesbian daughter. Clearly, the 53% of white women who voted for Donald Trump put aside whatever reservations they might have had about his character or attitudes toward women in general. Clinton's most iconic TV ad showing a young girl listening to Trump and asking mothers to consider the effect of a Trump presidency on their daughters, proved wide of the mark in attracting women voters to Clinton's cause. At best, it was an awkward way of reminding women of something they already knew. More importantly, it was trying to tap into a sense of group identity that in no way addressed any substantive concerns of young mothers, like support for childcare or higher wages for struggling families.

It is comforting to some Clinton voters to believe she lost because the core of Trump's appeal was racist and so now is the Republican Party. To cling to that illusion, however, is to ignore the fundamental fact that Trump's white working class support was a product of a deep disillusionment with both parties following the Great Recession and the elites that they represented. It is a dangerous illusion, for, as Dionne, Orenstein and Mann have written, "it ignores how winning a decent share of the white working class vote is essential for building a progressive coalition, particularly in the swing states in the Midwest" (ED 152).

If the fight for the Democratic nomination gets bogged down in a debate over to which Americans the party should appeal, it will be short-changing itself because Democratic programs are aimed at the common good and therefore should appeal to everyone who is thinking about the good of the country. Nobody, not the white working class, not the inhabitants of rural America, not the evangelicals who may also be deeply disturbed by Trump's border policy, not the traditional value conservatives tired of the many ways in which Trump has violated so many norms, not even the 1%, should be written off. The Democratic Party and its candidate should have something to say to all of them. There is no need to choose among favored groups and every reason, moral as well as political, not to.

* * *

Whatever happens, all roads ultimately lead back to the American people. There will always be another election, another edition of "America's choosing day" in Walt Whitman's wonderful phrase. In this spirit, let me end by sharing with you the last entry in my journal of the 2016 campaign, dated November 24. It serves to remind just how improbable our history has been and why so many still gather at our border:

> Today is Thanksgiving. Turkey will not be the central feature of all tables. Nicole Ponseca, a young woman whose parents immigrated to the United States in the 1960s and who has opened two Filipino restaurants in Brooklyn, will have prepared bibinka, a cake of rice flour, and coconut milk. Across the country, on the West Coast, in Alameda, California, Maura Passanisi will have made a potato casserole to honor the heritage of her Irish husband, she a descendant of 19th century Dutch immigrants. Meanwhile, in Junction City, Wisconsin, Diane Yang, the

eldest daughter of Laotian parents who gained asylum in the United States thirty years ago as Hmong refugees, will contribute her vermicelli egg roll stuffing to the family feast. And in Miami an eighty-year-old Margarita Velasco who came here at twenty-four in 1960 with her family as refugees from Cuba will have baked her pumpkin flan.

These were four of the fifteen individuals and recipes featured in last week's Food Section of *The New York Times*. Together they speak for a good kind of American exceptionalism; no other country on the planet has the richness of our family stories. No country's attempt to mold so many disparate groups into a functioning democracy is more audacious.

There are many strands to our history but certainly two of the most important are the immigrant struggle to make a new home and the African-American struggle to find freedom and happiness in a home they did not choose and in which they suffered for most of our history immense cruelties and discrimination.

Ours is a never-ending fight to both make our future better and make peace with our own past, a past that has been both glorious and ghastly, a past, to invoke William Faulkner's famous thought, that is never dead, "it's not even past." All we can do is our best. We don't always get it right. But we don't always get it wrong either.

References

References for Introduction, Chapters 1 and 2, and Appendix IV.

Abramowitz, Alan 2018. *The Great Alignment: Race, Party, Transformation and the Rise of Donald Trump.* Yale University Press.

Achen, Christopher and Larry Bartels 2017. *Democracy for Realists: Why Elections Do Not Produce Responsive Government.* Princeton: Princeton University Press.

Alexander, Dan "Trump's Decades Old Quotes Sound A Lot Like His Current Tweets" appearing in Forbes September 28, 2017 issue.

Allen Jonathan and Amie Parnes 2017. *Shattered: Inside Hillary Clinton's Doomed Campaign.* New York: Crown.

Bradlee, Ben Jr. 2018. *The Forgotten.* New York: Little Brown and Company.

Brooks, David "What is the Democratic Party's Story" appearing in The New York Times July 24, 2018.

Cassidy, John "Why is Trump in Michigan and Wisconsin". Appearing in The New Yorker October 26, 2016.

Ceaser, James W., Andrew E. Busch and John J. Pitney Jr. 2017. *Defying the Odds: The 2016 Election and American Politics.* New York: Rowman & Littlefield.

Chozick, Amy 2018. *Chasing Hillary: Ten Years, Two Presidential Campaigns and One Intact Glass Ceiling.* New York: Harper Collins.

Clinton, Hillary Rodham 2017. *What Happened.* New York: Simon & Schuster.

Coffey, Daniel J. and John C Green and David B. Cohen "The State of the Parties: Change and Continuity in 2016" appearing in *The State of the Parties 2018: The Changing Role of Contemporary American Political Parties* edited by John C. Green, Daniel J. Coffey and David B. Cohen 2018. New York: Rowman & Littlefield.

Collins, Gail 2012. *As Texas Goes...How the Lone Star State Hijacked the American Agenda.* New York: Norton/Liveright.

Dionne, E.J. Jr. and Norman J. Ornstein and Thomas E. Mann 2017 *One Nation After Trump.* New York: St. Martin's Press.

Durkin, Trish, email correspondence with author.

Fiorina, Morris P. 2017. *Unstable Majorities: Polarization, Party Sorting and Political Statements.* Stanford, California: Hoover Institution Press.

Genovese, Michael A. 2017. *Trumping American Politics: The Strange Case of the 2016 Presidential Election.* New York: Cambria Press.

Green, Joshua 2017. *Devil's Bargain.* Penguin Press.

Greenberg, Stanley "How She Lost" appearing in the September 21, 2017 issue of The American Prospect.

Hochschild, Arlie Russell 2016. *Strangers in their Own Land: Anger and Mourning on the American Right.* New York: The New Press.

Institute of Politics 2017. *Campaign for President: The Managers Look at 2016.* New York: Rowman & Littlefield.

Jacobson, Gary C. 2019. *Presidents and Parties in the Public Mind.* Chicago: University of Chicago Press.

Jamieson, Kathleen Hall 2018. *Cyber-War: How Russian Hackers and Trolls Helped Elect a President.* Oxford: Oxford University Press.

Johnson, Jenna "These Are the Towns That Love Donald Trump" appearing in the January 8, 2016 edition of the Washington Post.

Judis, John 2016. *The Populist Explosion: How the Great Recession Transformed American and European Politics.* Columbia Global Reports.

Kennedy, William 1993. *Riding the Yellow Trolley Car: Selected Nonfiction.* New York: Viking.

Kunhenn, Jim "This County was a Democratic Stronghold. Then Came Trump" appearing in the Washington Monthly, August 14, 2017.

Lyengar, Shanto appearing on podcast, part of the series "Why We Argue" hosted by the University of Connecticut's Humility and Conviction in Public Life Project.

Mansfield, Stephen 2017. *Choosing Donald Trump: God, Anger, Hope and Why Christian Conservatives Supported Him.* Grand Rapids, Michigan: Baker Books.

Mayer, Jane "How Russia Helped Sweep the Election for Trump" appearing in the September 24, 2018 issue of The New Yorker.

McCarty, Nolan and Keith T. Poole and Howard Rosenthal. 2016. *Polarized America: The Dance of Ideology and Unequal Riches.* Cambridge Mass.: MIT Press.

McElwee, Sean and Jason McDaniel "Fear of Diversity Made People More Likely to Vote Trump" appearing in The Nation for March 14, 2017.

Mutz, Diana C. "Status Threat, Not Economic Hardship, explains the 2016 Presidential Vote." Proceedings of the National Academy of Sciences 2018.

Noonan, Peggy "What to Tell Your Children About Trump" appearing in The Wall Street Journal, November 18, 2016.

Oliver, J. Eric and Thomas J. Wood 2018. *Enchanted America: How Intuition and Reason Divide Our Politics.* Chicago: University of Chicago Press.

Owen, Diana "Tipping the Balance of Power in Elections? Voters Engagement in the Digital Campaign" appearing in *The Internet and the 2016 Presidential Campaign*, Jody C. Baumgartner and Terri L. Towner (editors) 2017. Lexington Books.

Patterson, Richard North 2016. *Fever Swamp: A Journey Through the Strange Neverland of the 2016 Presidential Race*. New York: Quercus.

Pollak, Joel and Larry Schweikart 2017. *How Trump Won: the Inside Story of a Revolution*. Regnery Publishing.

Sabato, Larry J. "The 2016 Election That Broke All, or At Least Most, of the Rules" appearing in *Trumped* 2017, Larry J. Sabato, Kyle Kondik, Geoffrey Skelley (editors). New York: Rowman & Littlefield.

Saul, Josh "Why Did Donald Trump Win? Just Visit Luzerne County" appearing in the online edition of Newsweek Magazine on December 5, 2016.

Schaffner, Brian F., Matthew MacWilliams and TatishiNteta "Explaining White Polarization in the 2016 Vote for President: The Sobering Role of Racism and Sexism" https://people.umass.edu/schaffne/schaffner_et_al_IDC_conference.pdf

Sexton, Jared Yates 2017. *The People Are Going to Rise Like the Waters Upon Your Shore: A Story of American Rage*. Berkeley, California: Counterpoint.

Skocpol, Theda and Vanessa Williamson 2016 *"The Tea Party and the Remaking of Republican Conservatism* New York: Oxford University Press.

Sides, John and Michael Tesler and Lynn Vavreck 2018. *Identity Crisis: The 2016 Presidential Campaign and the Battle for the Meaning of America*. Princeton: Princeton University Press.

Sifry, Micah L. "Obama's Lost Army" appearing in The New Republic, February 9, 2017.

Silver, Nate "The Comey Letter Probably Cost Clinton the Election" May 3, 2017. The FiveThirtyEight website.

Silver, Nate "How Much Did Russian Intelligence Affect the 2016 Election" February 18, 2018. The FiveThirtyEight website.

Spicer, Sean 2018. *The Briefing: Politics, the Press and the President*. Washington D.C.: Regnery Publishing.

Starr, Paul 2019. *Entrenchment: Wealth, Power, and the Consti-tution of Democratic Societies.* New Haven: Yale University Press.

Steger Wayne "Populist Challenges and the 2016 Presidential Nominations" appearing in *The 2016 Presidential Election: The Causes and Consequences of a Political Earthquake* edited by Amnori Cavari, Richard J. Powell, and Kenneth R. Mayer 2017. New York: Lexington Books.

Tur, Katy 2017. *Unbelievable: My Front Row Street to the Craziest Campaign in American History.* Dey Street Books.

Warren, Elizabeth 2017. *This Fight is Our Fight: The Battle to Save America's Middle Class.* New York: Henry Holt and Company. Metropolitan Books.

Wead, Doug 2017. *Game of Thorns.* New York: Hachette Book Group.

Wear, Michael "Why Did Obama Win More White Evangelical Votes Than Clinton" found on washingtonpost.com, posted on November 22, 2016.

Wood, Dan with Soren Jordan 2017. *Party Polarization in America: The War Over Two Social Contracts.* Cambridge: Cambridge University Press.

Zito, Salena and Brad Todd   2018. *The Great Revolt: Inside the Populist Coalition Reshaping American Politics.* Crow.

References for Chapter 3

Bradlee, Ben Jr. 2018. *The Forgotten.* New York: Little Brown and Company.

Brooks, David "Do You Have To Be a Jerk to Be Great" appearing in the July 30, 2019 issue of the New York Times.

Fallows, Deborah and James Fallows 2018. *Our Towns: A 100,000-Mile Journey into the Heart of America.* Pantheon.

Friedman, Thomas "The Answers to Our Problems Aren't as Simple as Left or Right" appearing in The New York Times, July 23, 2019.

Harpine, William D. "Social Media in the 2016 Presidential and Vice Presidential Debates" appearing in *Televised Presidential Debates in a Changing Media Environment, Volume 2: The Citizens Talk Back.* Edward A. Hinck, Editor. Praeger.

Hershey, Marjorie "The Media" appearing in *The Elections of 2016,* Michael nelson (editor) Los Angeles: Sage CO Press.

Hochschild, Arlie Russell 2016. *Strangers in their Own Land: Anger and Mourning on the American Right.* New York: The New Press.

Jennings, Freddie J. and Mitchell S. McKinney and Molly M. Greenwood. "Preaching to the Choir: Partisan Social Identity and Presidential Debate Social Watching" appearing in *Televised Presidential Debates in a Changing Media Environment, Volume 2: The Citizens Talk Back.* Edward A. Hinck, Editor. Praeger.

Klarman, Michael "Trump, the Republican Party and the Rule of Law" appearing on April 5, 2019 in the Harvard Law School, Rule of Law Blog.

Lyengar, Shanto appearing on podcast, part of the series "Why We Argue" hosted by the University of Connecticut's Humility and Conviction in Public Life Project.

Skowronek, Stephen 2011. *Political Leadership in Political Time: Reprise and Reappraisal - Second Edition, Revised and Expanded.* University Press of Kansas.

Teles, Steven July 18, 2019. "First Thoughts on Yuval Levin's Address To the Conference on National Conservatism". https://niskanencenter. org/...first-thoughts-on-yuval-levine-address-to-the-conference

References for Chapter 4

Alter, Jonathan "Roosevelt's Complicated Liberalism appearing in *The New York Times,* June 22, 2019 at page A23.

Cohen, Lizabeth "A Market Failure In Affordable Housing" appearing in the July 10, 2019 edition of *The New York Times* at page A27.

Dionne, E.J. Jr. and Norman J. Ornstein and Thomas E. Mann 2017 One Nation After Trump. New York: St. Martin's Press.

Ghilarducci, Teresa "Five Good Reasons It Doesn't Feel Like The Trump Tax Cut Benefited You" Forbes Magazine April 9, 2019.

Gingrich, Newt 2018. *Trump's America: The Truth About Our Nation's Great Comeback.* New York, Nashville: Center Press.

Kessler, Andy in his Opinion, Inside View column appearing in the April 22, 2019 edition of *The Wall Street Journal.*

Meyerson, Harold "Climate Change and the Democrats" appearing in The American *Prospect*, Summer 2019 issue.

Noonan, Peggy "If Biden Runs, They'll Tear Him Up" appearing in the April 6-7 2019 edition of *The Wall Street Journal* at A13.

Saul, Stephanie and Jeremy W. Peters "Where 'Go Back' Attack Finds Sympathetic Ears" appearing in the July 23, 2019 issue of The New York Times.

Span, Paula "Long on Care Needed. Short on Cash Necessary." appearing in *The New York Times*, May 14, 2019, page D5.

Tavernise, Sabrina "These Americans Are Done with Politics" appearing in the November 17, 2018 edition of *The New York Times.*

Waldman, Paul "The 'Electability' Claim is swallowing up the Democratic primaries but it's Nonsense" appearing May 3 in www.washingtonpost.com/blogs/plum-line/

The WinstonGroupwww.winstongroup.net "Focus on OUR Concerns: An Analysis of the 2018 Midterm Elections

Appendix I: Excerpts from Announcement Speeches of Hillary Clinton and Donald J. Trump.

A Brief Comment:

Hillary Clinton delivered her announcement on June 13, 2015 at Franklin D. Roosevelt Four Freedoms Park on Roosevelt Island in New York City. Donald Trump delivered his three days later at Trump Tower in Manhattan.

They make fascinating reading. Hillary's was filled with progressive idealism painting a picture of a problem-solving nation that would harness the talents of all of its people. She described four fights that would mark her presidency but it was only two — "to make the economy work for everyday Americans" and "to strengthen American families" — that took up almost the entire speech (The other two — to work for peace and global security and to revitalize our democracy — seemed almost afterthoughts.) She attacked the Republicans for being the party of yesterday interested primarily in preserving the status quo for wealthy Americans. She would fight, among other things, for pre-k for every child in America and paid family leave. All in all, it was clear she envisioned a traditional presidential election: a centrist liberal versus a centrist conservative. The idea of running against someone like Donald Trump was probably the furthest thing from her mind.

Donald's speech was the exact opposite of Hillary's. Where she occasionally strayed from her carefully structured text, he occasionally looked down at something probably resembling a grocery list. It might or might not have been graced with the stray verb. It may have been the first stream of consciousness announcement in American history. Yet it would anticipate every major theme in his campaign, except his vilification of Hillary.

I am sure I enjoyed and approved of Hillary's speech. Indeed, reading it now makes me regret even more her loss, for she was clearly trying to reach out to the entire nation with proposals that made sense and in some cases could even possibly win Republican support. Unfortunately, I'm also sure that even a day later I could not remember a single line from the speech. Trump's speech, on the other hand, was impossible to forget. It wasn't just the anti-immigrant rant. There is something to be said for simple declarative sentences. "The greatest social program is a job." "We need somebody to make the brand of America great again." "I will be the greatest jobs president God ever created."

And his gift for exaggeration that somehow still made his point was on full display. He predicted that if Obama made his deal with Iran, "Israel maybe won't exist very long." Attacking Obamacare, he quoted a doctor friend who said "I have more accountants than nurses." He described how Republicans, now his rivals, came to him asking for his support. He said he liked them but none of them were talking about the things that mattered. And then he made the connection that Sanders supporters would have fully embraced. Today's politicians, Democrats and Republicans, were "all talk and no action." "They will not bring us to the promised land" because they are all "controlled by the lobbyists, by the donors, and the special interests." Virtually every substantive point he made was accompanied by some kind of anecdote or personal comment. It would be vintage Trump for the rest of the campaign.

Hillary Clinton

Advances in technology and the rise of global trade have created whole new areas of economic activity and opened new markets for our exports, but they have also displaced jobs and undercut wages for millions of Americans. The financial industry and many multinational corporations have created huge wealth for a few by focusing too much on short-term profit and too little on long-term value... too much on complex trading schemes and stock buy-backs, too little on investments in new businesses, jobs, and fair compensation. Our political system is so paralyzed by gridlock and dysfunction that most Americans have lost confidence that anything can actually get done. And they've lost trust in the ability of both government and Big Business to change course. Now, we can blame historic forces beyond our control for some of this, but the choices we've made as a nation, leaders and citizens alike, have also played a big role. Our next President must work with Congress and every other willing partner across our entire country. And I will do just that — to turn the tide so these currents start working for us more than against us...

In the coming weeks, I'll propose specific policies to: reward businesses who invest in long term value rather than the quick buck — because that leads to higher growth for the economy, higher wages for workers, and yes, bigger profits, everybody will have a better time. I will rewrite the tax code so it rewards hard work and investments here at home, not quick trades or stashing profits overseas. I will give new incentives to companies that give their employees a fair share of the profits their hard work earns. We will unleash a new generation of entrepreneurs and small business owners by providing tax relief, cutting red tape, and making it easier to get a small business loan. We will restore America to the cutting edge of innovation, science, and research by increasing both public and private investments. And we will make America the clean energy superpower of the 21st century…

In America, every family should feel like they belong. So we should offer hard-working, law-abiding immigrant families a path to citizenship. Not second-class status. And, we should ban discrimination against LGBT Americans and their families so they can live, learn, marry, and work just like everybody else. You know, America's diversity, our openness, our devotion to human rights and freedom is what's drawn so many to our shores. What's inspired people all over the world. I know. I've seen it with my own eyes…

Well, I may not be the youngest candidate in this race. But I will be the youngest woman President in the history of the United States! And the first grandmother as well. And one additional advantage: You're won't see my hair turn white in the White House. I've been coloring it for years! So I'm looking forward to a great debate among Democrats, Republicans, and Independents. I'm not running to be a President only for those Americans who already agree with me. I want to be a President for all

Americans. And along the way, I'll just let you in on this little secret. I won't get everything right. Lord knows I've made my share of mistakes. Well, there's no shortage of people pointing them out! And I certainly haven't won every battle I've fought. But leadership means perseverance and hard choices. You have to push through the setbacks and disappointments and keep at it.I think you know by now that I've been called many things by many people — 'quitter' is not one of them.

Donald Trump

Wow. Whoa. That is some group of people. Thousands. So nice, thank you very much. That's really nice. Thank you. It's great to be at Trump Tower… There's been no crowd like this.

Our country is in serious trouble. We don't have victories anymore. We used to have victories, but we don't have them. When was the last time anybody saw us beating, let's say, China in a trade deal? They kill us. I beat China all the time.

The U.S. has become a dumping ground for everybody else's problems. Thank you. It's true, and these are the best and the finest. When Mexico sends its people, they're not sending their best. They're not sending you. They're not sending you. They're sending people that have lots of problems, and they're bringing those problems with us. They're bringing drugs. They're bringing crime. They're rapists. And some, I assume, are good people. But I speak to border guards and they tell us what we're getting. We spent $2 trillion in Iraq, $2 trillion. We lost thousands of lives, thousands in Iraq. We have wounded soldiers, who I love, I love — they're great — all over the place, thousands and thousands of wounded soldiers. And we have nothing. We can't even go there. We have nothing...

Our real unemployment is anywhere from 18 to 20 percent. Don't believe the 5.6. Don't believe it. But the real number, the real number is anywhere from 18 to 19 and maybe even 21 percent, and nobody talks about it, because it's a statistic that's full of nonsense.

Now, our country needs— our country needs a truly great leader, and we need a truly great leader now. We need a leader that wrote *The Art of the Deal*. We need a leader that can bring back our jobs, can bring back our manufacturing, can bring back our military, can take care of our vets. Our vets have been abandoned.

I like China. I sell apartments for — I just sold an apartment for $15 million to somebody from China. Am I supposed to dislike them? I own a big chunk of the Bank of America Building at 1290 Avenue of the Americas that I got from China in a war. Very valuable. I love China..... We have all the cards, but we don't know how to use them. We don't even know that we have the cards, because our leaders don't understand the game. We could turn off that spigot by charging them tax until they behave properly.

If I was [*sic*] president, I'd say [to Ford's CEO], "Congratulations. I understand that you're building a nice $2.5 billion car factory in Mexico and that you're going to take your cars and sell them to the United States zero tax, just flow them across the border."...So I would say, "Congratulations. That's the good news. Let me give you the bad news. Every car and every truck and every part manufactured in this plant that comes across the border, we're going to charge you a 35-percent tax… So I have a total net worth, and now with the increase, it'll be well-over $10 billion…..I'm not doing that to brag, because you know what? I don't have to brag. I don't have to, believe it or not.

If we have another three or four years — you know, we're at $18 trillion [national debt] now. We're soon going to be at $20 trillion. According to the economists— who I'm not big believers in, but, nevertheless, this is what they're saying— that $24 trillion— we're very close— that's the point of no return. $24 trillion. We will be there soon. That's when we become Greece. That's when we become a country that's unsalvageable. And we're gonna be there very soon. We're gonna be there very soon.

Sadly, the American dream is dead. But if I get elected president I will bring it back bigger and better and stronger than ever before, and we will make America great again.

Appendix II: Excerpts from Announcement Speeches of Three Leading Democratic Candidates in 2020

Elizabeth Warren

We are here to take on a fight that will shape our lives, our children's lives and our grandchildren's lives just as surely as the fight that began in these streets more than a century ago. Because the man in the White House is not the cause of what is broken, he is just the latest and most extreme symptom of what's gone wrong in America, a product of a rigged system that props up the rich and powerful and kicks dirt on everyone else. So once he's gone, we can't pretend that none of this ever happened. It won't be enough to just undo the terrible acts of this administration. We can't afford just to tinker around the edges of a tax credit here, a regulation there. Our fight is for big structural change.

This is the fight of our lives; the fight to build an America where dreams are possible and America that works for everyone. And that is why I stand here today to declare that I am a candidate for President of the United States of America.

In the 1940s, 90 percent of all kids were destined to do better than their parents. By the 1980s, the odds slipped to 50/50, and now we could be the first generation in American history where more kids do worse than their parents. And meanwhile, the rich and powerful seem to break the rules and pay no price, no matter what they did. They grow richer and more powerful. Bailouts for bankers that cheat. Tax cuts for companies that scam. Subsidies for corporations that pollute. That's what a rigged system looks like. Too little accountability for the rich. too little opportunity for everyone else.

End lobbying as we know it... Make justices of the United States Supreme Court follow a basic code of ethics... Ban members of Congress from trading stocks... make every single candidate for federal office put their taxes online. Make it quick and easy to join a union. Break up monopolies when they choke off competition. Take on Wall Street banks so the big banks can never again threaten the security of our economy. When giant corporations and their leaders cheat their customers, stomp out their competitors and rob their workers, let's prosecute them.

I'm tired of hearing that we can't afford to make investments in things that create economic opportunities for families. I'm tired of hearing that we can't afford to make investments in things like housing and opioid treatment — can't afford to address things like rural neglect or the legacy of racial discrimination. I'm tired of hearing what we can't afford because it's just not true. We are the wealthiest nation in the history of the world. Of course we can afford these investments.

We also need to end the unwritten rule of politics that says that anyone who wants to run for office has to start by sucking up to a bunch of rich donors on Wall Street and powerful insiders in Washington. So, I'm opting out of that rule. I'm not taking a dime of PAC money in this campaign,

We all want a country where everyone, not just the wealthy, everyone, can take care of their families. We all want a country where every American, not just the ones who hire armies of lobbyists and lawyers, everyone can participate in democracy; a country where every child can dream big and reach for real opportunity and we are in the fight to build an America that works for everyone.

So look, I get it. I get it. This won't be easy. Now there are a lot of people out there with money and power and armies of lobbyists and lawyers. People who are prepared to spend more money than you and I could ever dream of to stop us from making any of these solutions a reality. People who will say it's extreme or radical to demand an America where every family has some economic security and every kid has a real opportunity to succeed and I say to them, get ready, because change is coming faster than you think.

The textile workers here in Lawrence more than 100 years ago won their fight because they refused to be divided. Today, we gather on those same streets, ready to stand united again. This is our moment in history. The moment we're called to. This is our moment to dream big, fight hard and win. Thank you.

Joe Biden

Folks, thank you, Jill. I'm Joe Biden, and I'm Jill's husband. You all think I'm kidding. That's how I'm identified. Everyone knows Jill is a Philadelphia girl. She loves this city. I do, too. But to paraphrase the poet, James Joyce, I have to say this, folks, because I'm near my state, when I die, "Delaware" will be written on my heart.

But I love Philly. Look, I'm mildly prejudice, but I think she made a great, great second lady, and she's going to make one heck of a first lady.

This campaign is just getting started. And I promise you this, no one, no one is going to work longer, no one is going to campaign harder to win your hearts, your trust, and your support than the son of Catherine Eugenia Finnegan from Scranton, Pennsylvania, and Joseph R. Biden from Delaware.

You will not hear me speak — I made a pledge. I mean this sincerely. You will not hear me speak ill of another Democrat.

Our Constitution doesn't begin with the phrase, "We the Democrats" or "We the Republicans." And it certainly doesn't begin with the phrase, "We the Donors."

Look, it [the phrase We the People] began with the phrase that stands for we are all in this together. We need to remember that today I think more than any time in my career. Our politics has become so mean, so petty, so negative, so partisan, so angry, and so unproductive — so unproductive. Instead of debating our opponents, we demonize them. Instead of questioning judgments, we question their motives. Instead of listening, we shout. Instead of looking for solutions, we look to score political points.

But no more. No more. Because this politics, this politics is pulling us apart. It's ripping this country apart at the seams. Our politicians, our politics today, traffics in division, and our president is the divider in chief.

Look, but he's not the only one. Far from it. He is just the worst practitioner of politics that singles out, scapegoats, and demonizes. He holds the other as the source of all the problems. You hear it — the immigrant, the Muslim, anyone different in creed or color or conviction, they're the problem. That's what he says. That's been the scheme used by unscrupulous politicians for decades.

But it comes at a gigantic cost. I mean this from the bottom of my heart, it comes at a gigantic cost. It weakens us. It distracts us. It divides us. It causes us to lose credibility around the world. It picks at the wound, and it solves nothing. This is not who we are.

I absolutely refuse to accept the notion that that's who we have to be. Folks, in this country, we're all bound together in this great experiment of equality and opportunity and decency. We haven't lived up, and we've never given up on it. Everyone, and I mean everyone, everyone is in on the deal. That's why we've been the beacon of hope for the rest of the world. That's why the world has always looked at us.

America guarantees everyone, and I mean everyone, be treated with dignity. America gives hate no safe harbor. Folks, that's what we believe. That's who we are. And I believe America has always been at its best when

America has acted as one America, one America. One America may be a simple notion, but it doesn't make it any less profound. This nation needs to come together. It has to come together.

Folks, I know some of the really smart folks say Democrats don't want to hear about unity. They say Democrats are so angry, that the angrier a candidate can be, the better chance he or she has to win the Democratic nomination. Well, I don't believe it. I really don't. If Democrats — I believe Democrats want to unify this nation. That's what our party has always been about.

So let me be real clear, everybody listen, Democrats and Republicans, if I'm elected your president, I'm going to do whatever it takes to make progress on the matters that matter most — civil liberties, civil rights, voting rights, women's right to choose, national security, personal security, health care, an economy that rewards work, not just wealth, a climate change policy that will save our children and grandchildren and this planet.

Look, I know there are times — I know there are times when only a bare-knuckle fight will do. I know we have to take on Republicans to do what's right without any help from them. That's what it took to pass the Affordable Care Act.

Folks, we need a 21st century strategy for America. But every tool that Donald Trump uses is out of the past. Folks, we have to get focused, focused on the future. It's only the way we're going to invest in educational system. Our people need to succeed in the 21st century. Jill always says — she's a community college professor — she always says, any country that out-educates us will out out-compete us. That's a natural fact.

Folks, that success will come when we generate free community colleges, invest in job training and apprenticeships, continue education, allowing people to fill jobs of the future, a stronger commitment to pre-K, and so much more. Folks, we know it works. We know what we have to do. So let's stop fighting and start fixing.

Folks, it is the only way we're going to deal with the existential crisis posed by climate change. There's not much time left. We need a clean energy revolution. We need it now. We have to start now. We have to move on what we've already built.

And by the way, we have to stop the thinking that clean energy and job creation don't go together. They do. They do...

Folks, everybody knows who Donald Trump is. Even his supporters know who he is. But I have to let you know, here's the deal, we have to let them know who we are, what we stand for. We choose hope over fear, truth over lies and, yes, unity over division. So folks, it's time for us to lift our heads up, open our hearts, and remember who we are. We are the United States of America. I mean this, there's not a single thing we cannot do if we do it together. God bless you all, and may God protect our troops. Thank you, thank you, thank you.

Kamala Harris

My mother used to say "don't sit around and complain about things, do something." Basically I think she was saying. You've got to get up and stand up and don't give up the fight!

And it is this deep-rooted belief that inspired me to become a lawyer and a prosecutor.

It was just a couple blocks from this very spot that nearly 30 years ago as a young district attorney I walked into the courtroom for the very first time and said the five words that would guide my life's work:

"Kamala Harris, for the people."

Now, I knew our criminal justice system was deeply flawed. But I also knew the profound impact law enforcement has on people's lives, and it's responsibility to give them safety and dignity...

You see, in our system of justice, we believe that a harm against any one of us is a har against all of us. That's why when we file a case, it's not filed in the name of the victim. It reads, "The People"...

When we have leaders who lie and bully and attack a free press and undermine our democratic institutions that's not our America. When white supremacists march and murder in Charlottesville or massacre innocent worshipers at a Pittsburgh synagogue that's not our America. When we have children in cages crying for their mothers and fathers, don't you dare call it border security, that's a human rights abuse and that's not our America. When we have leaders who attack public schools and vilify public school teachers that's not our America. When bankers who crashed our economy get bonuses but workers who brought our country back can't even get a raise that's not our America.

I'm running for president because I love my country. I love my country. I'm running to be president, of the people, by the people, and for all people. I'm running to fight for an America where the economy works for working people. For an America where you only have to work one job to pay the bills, where hard work is rewarded and where any worker can join a union.

I am running to declare, once and for all, that health care is a fundamental right, and we will deliver that right with Medicare for All! I am running to declare education is a fundamental right, and we will guarantee that right with universal pre-K and debt free college! I am running to guarantee working and middle class families an overdue pay increase. We will deliver the largest working and middle-class tax cut in a generation. Up to $500 a month to help America's families make ends meet.

And we'll pay for it by reversing this administration's give always to big corporations and the top one percent...

I'm running to fight for an America where no mother or father has to teach their young son that people may stop him, arrest him, chase him, or kill him, because of his race. An America where every parent can send their children to school without being haunted by the horror of another killing spree. Where we treat attacks on voting rights and civil rights and women's rights and immigrant rights as attacks on our country itself. An America where we welcome refugees and bring people out of the shadows, and provide a pathway to citizenship. An America where our daughters, where our sisters, where our mothers and grandmothers are respected where they live and where they work. Where reproductive rights are not just protected by the Constitution of the United States but guaranteed in every state. I'll fight for an America where we keep our word and where we honor our promises. Because that's our America. That's the America I believe in. That's the America I know we believe in.

As Robert Kennedy many years ago said, "Only those who dare to fail greatly can ever achieve greatly."He also said, "I do not lightly dismiss the dangers and the difficulties of challenging an incumbent President, but these are not ordinary times and this is not an ordinary election." He said, "At stake is not simply the leadership of our party and even our country. It is our right to moral leadership of this planet."

Appendix III: State Election Polls in Swing States in the 10 days before the 2016 Presidential Election

A major question after the 2016 election was how the polls got it so wrong. Actually, the national polls did not get it wrong. Most predicted a fairly close popular vote margin with Clinton the favorite. Nationally, that is exactly what happened, the national polls showing on average a margin of 3% for Hillary; her ultimate popular vote margin was roughly 2%.

State polls in the rust belt states did get it wrong and the result for Clinton was catastrophic; the blue wall did not hold. In May 2017, the American Association for Public Opinion Research issued a detailed report evaluating the 2016 polling. In looking for explanations for the under-estimation of the support for Trump, the Executive Summary of the Report found the most evidence for:

> **"Real change in vote preference during the final week or so of the campaign.** About 13 percent of voters in Wisconsin, Florida and Pennsylvania decided on their presidential vote choice in the final week, according to the best available data. These voters broke for Trump by near 30 points in

Wisconsin and by 17 points in Florida and Pennsylvania.

Adjusting for over-representation of college graduates was critical, but many polls did not do it. In 2016 there was a strong correlation between education and presidential vote in key states. Voters with higher education levels were more likely to support Clinton. Furthermore, recent studies are clear that people with more formal education are significantly more likely to participate in surveys than those with less education. Many polls — especially at the state level — did not adjust their weights to correct for the over-representation of college graduates in their surveys, and the result was over-estimation of support for Clinton.

Some Trump voters who participated in pre-election polls did not reveal themselves as Trump voters until after the election, and they outnumbered late-revealing Clinton voters. This finding could be attributable to either late deciding or misreporting (the so-called *Shy Trump* effect) in the pre-election polls. A number of other tests for the Shy Trump theory yielded no evidence to support it." (Report's Emphases)

Below is a comparison of the RealClear Politics average for all the state-wide polls conducted in each of the 2016 battleground states in roughly the last seven to ten days of the campaign compared to the actual results on election day 2016.

Wisconsin: 7.2% discrepancy (projected Clinton margin 6.5%; Trump actual margin 0.7%)

Iowa: 6.5% discrepancy (projected Trump margin 3%; actual margin 9.5%)

Ohio: 5.9% discrepancy (projected Trump margin 2.2%; actual margin 8.1%).

Michigan: 3.9% discrepancy (projected Clinton margin 3.6%; Trump actual margin 0.3%)

Nevada: 3.2% discrepancy (projected Trump margin 0.8%; actual Clinton margin 2.4%)

Pennsylvania: 2.8% discrepancy (projected Clinton margin 2.1%; actual Trump margin 0.7%)

North Carolina: 2.8% discrepancy (projected Trump margin 0.8%; actual margin 3.6%)

Colorado: 1.9% discrepancy (projected Clinton margin 3.0%; actual margin 4.9%)

Florida: 0.8% discrepancy (projected Trump margin 0.4%; actual margin 1.2%)

Arizona: 0.5% discrepancy (projected Trump margin 4.0%; actual margin 3.5%)

Virginia: 0.1% discrepancy (projected Clinton margin 5.3%; actual margin 5.4%)

New Hampshire No discrepancy (projected Clinton margin 0.3%; actual margin 0.3%)

Appendix IV – Additional Perspectives on Polarization

The work of Wood and Jordan seems to find indirect support in a book titled *Polarized America* in which the three authors (Nolan McCarty, Keith Poole and Howard Rosenthal) show how the most recent polarization of the two parties has tracked with growing income inequality and the influx of low-skilled labor into the United States following the Immigration Act of 1965. The growing inequality has, of course many causes, including, as McCarty et al. point out, how higher education has become a prerequisite for a high quality of life in the new economy, the decline of labor unions, globalization, excessive executive compensation, and high rates of divorce. The authors found that as incomes grow, voters tend to identify more with the Republican Party as the natural champions of the Founders/Old Guard Contract described by Wood/Jordan. They also question the widely accepted claim that many evangelicals, for example, vote against their economic interest in voting Republican, showing quite clearly that "for born-again Christians and evangelicals, the percentage of Republican increases with income" (NM 103). The findings of McCarty et al and Wood/Jordan dovetail nicely.

James Ceaser, Andrew Busch, and John Pitney Jr. in their study of the 2016 election offer still another view of the electorate. They emphasize that roughly half of the electorate defines itself as moderate or do not place themselves on any ideological scale at all (JC 172). For them, "group identities and group attitudes are the growing force behind affective polarization in American politics." They argue that "people tend to understand politics in terms of group interests and group identities, and voters often act on group-based attitudes" (Id). For these individuals, "the most important group identity in politics is party identification" and party identification itself "shapes other political attitudes and behavior." Their emphasis on group behavior fits well with a current media and social environment that naturally encourages people to sort themselves into the like-minded. They, like Abramowitz, emphasize attitudes toward race and immigration in shaping party identification.

Let me add one other factor to the mix. My own belief is that the infrastructure of today's politics – the non-competitive nature of so many congressional districts resulting from partisan and incumbent gerrymandering and the constant need for money – also has contributed to polarization in the House of Representatives which in turn has a kind of feedback mechanism that helps lead to polarization among the electorate. As has been widely observed, many congressional districts are now so clearly the province of one party or the other that their representatives worry much more about primary than general election challenges. This means that Republican representatives must always protect their right flank and Democrats their left — often leaving little incentive for compromise.

We are a long time from the phenomenon of the 1890 and 1894 Congressional elections when in 1890 the Republicans lost 85 seats only to gain back 120 seats four years later. The total of 120 seats represented fully one-third of the then membership of 357 Representatives. Today, a comparable election result would require 143 seats to change hands, an event as likely to happen as Elvis returning to the building. I might add that with the House of Representatives capped by law at 435 members, members of Congress today, with increasing population, now represent on average of 747,000 persons; in 1910, the figure was 210,000. Thus, the number of voters who have been effectively disenfranchised by gerrymandered districts keeps growing and growing.

I should add that the authors of *Polarized America* do not share my view of gerrymandering's effect on polarization. Without getting too deeply into the weeds for what is a complex question, let me just offer the following. Suppose that tomorrow all congressional districts had to be configured, as much as possible, to have an equal number of Democrats and Republicans. Does anyone doubt that such elections would produce candidates closer to the center since obviously no candidate could simply rely on getting out its base given the number of independents and party moderates. So clearly, the more politicians are allowed to veer from this standard toward non-competitiveness, the less vital is it for them to seek ways to gravitate toward the center.

With respect to the impact of campaign finance on polarization, though I'm not aware of any studies on the ideological make-up of large contributors as opposed to the rank-and-file, I suspect that they are more generally ideological in their make-up and this will also have an impact in how candidates articulate their positions. After all, if money is the lifeblood of politics and you need to rely on the more ideological spectrum of the party for that sustenance, it isn't hard to figure out to whose opinions your average representative will be most sensitive. This is particularly significant given how much time incumbents devote to raising money. Senator Elizabeth Warren has asserted, "…it's probably accurate to say that candidates and members of Congress generally spend 30 to 70 percent of their time raising money" (EW164). Warren also reminds us that when Congressman Steven Israel retired in 2016 he explained, "I don't think I can spend another day in another call room making another call begging for money" (EW 165).

Appendix V: Memories – 1952 and 1960.

During the 2016 election, I kept a detailed journal of the 2016 presidential campaign. Occasionally, I would think back to 1960 and the presidential election that year contested by John F. Kennedy of Massachusetts and Richard M. Nixon of California. It was the election that ignited my interest in politics. What follows are four journal entries in which nostalgia got the better of me. The first one actually goes back to 1952 and a trip to the local Democratic campaign headquarters. The other three are about the 1960 election.

Journal Entry for August 19 (A 1952 visit to Democratic headquarters)

This is a relatively quiet time in the [2016] campaign, both sides preparing for battle. It has given me the chance to recall my first memories of a political campaign. That would have been in 1952, Eisenhower v. Stevenson. It was not exactly a fair fight, as it pitted a hero General, the leader of the Allied forces on D-Day against a divorced bachelor governor of Illinois. It was an important election, ending the twenty-year control of the Democrats over the White House. Eisenhower, not much respected by liberals at the time, would, as President, accept most of the New Deal and inaugurate the interstate highway system.

He would also refuse to enter into the Vietnam conflict. His campaign centered on his pledge to end the war in Korea and to fight the Communists more effectively than the Democrats who, the Republicans charged, had "lost" China to the communists in 1949.

At age seven I was aware of none of this. What I do remember is visiting our local Democratic campaign headquarters with my mother. It was a simple storefront on one of the two main streets in Plainfield, New Jersey, a bedroom community served by the Jersey Central line, its huge Black locomotives (just like the one for my Lionel train) carrying its daily cargo of professional and business-men into Manhattan. The "headquarters" shared space on the first floor with a dental office and consisted simply of a large room with two long, standard issue collapsible tables – the kind you would use for an outdoor barbecue – hugging the back wall. This was clearly not a permanent operation nor one with great expectations. Plainfield was a Republican town. In the room are three people: a large elderly lady with blue hair behind the tables, my mother and myself. We were the only ones in the place. No com-puters. No telephones. I could have been at the library.
In my mind's eye, I see my mother bending over the table examining some of the campaign literature. It must have been mid October because I remember leaves blowing against the storefront window.

One thing did catch my seven-year old fancy that autumn day. A button. A button that seemed to me a technological marvel because you could manipulate it so it would show alternating images, one simply a plea to "Vote for Adlai," the other an image of the candidate himself. How do they do that? I wondered, a question I have been asking ever since as one technological marvel succeeds another in altering our daily lives.

Adlai Stevenson was the darling of the liberals in 1952 but his Vice-Presidential candidate was the staunch segregationist, Senator John Sparkman of Alabama, and the only states that Stevenson carried in the Eisenhower landslide were the deep South (Arkansas, Louisiana, Mississippi, Alabama, Georgia, South Carolina and North Carolina) and two border states (Kentucky and West Virginia).

My parents much admired Stevenson for his wit and eloquence. Eisenhower, as President, was known for his adventures with syntax during his press conference but he was trusted and admired. Historians, particularly recent historians, have been much kinder to Eisenhower, deservedly so I believe, than my parents.

Journal Entry for September 6
(I interview Senator Goldwater)

The [2016] campaign has truly begun. In Tampa, Clinton continued her attacks on Trump, focusing on a $25,000 donation that Trump made to the campaign of the then Florida Attorney General Pam Bondi who was investigating Trump University. Meanwhile, Trump, in an interview with ABC, claimed, "Well, I just don't think she has a presidential look, and you need a presidential look."

I wonder whether I would have gotten as interested in politics and history as I did in 1960 had the race I was exposed to then been this one, not the Kennedy-Nixon clash. I found the race so enthralling, I thought I would write a book about it.

It was a much different time and so, in April 1962, my fairly protective parents allowed me to go to Washington by myself and spend a week at the YMCA not far from the White House. Earlier, I had written to a number of U.S. Senators and Representatives asking if I might interview them about the 1960 presidential election. It turned out that what I thought might be a disaster – that my school's Easter recess coincided with Congress' — was a blessing in disguise.

I particularly wanted to interview Barry Goldwater who was already entering stage right of national politics and Frank Church who had delivered the keynote speech at the Democratic convention. For some reason, unlike most of their colleagues, both men were still in Washington. I would start each day that week going to Senator Goldwater's office and each day, a kindly elderly secretary by the name of Edna Coerver would tell me the Senator was not in but I shouldn't give up. I had really given up hope but on my last morning in Washington, she smiled and ushered me into the Senator's office. You must understand that the Senate Office Building was eerily empty with almost everyone gone. The Senator himself was about to leave and I had come at probably the only moment he could give me. He couldn't have been more gracious. I still remember the model planes that lined his office; I also remember how critical he was of Nixon's decision to put Henry Cabot Lodge on the ticket as his Vice-President. We talked for more than half an hour, a sixteen-year-old New Jersey public high school kid and potentially the next President of the United States. Not likely to happen today.

Goldwater would turn out to be a different kind of conservative, one who in later years would take on the religious right of his party on many issues, among them gay rights. "You don't have to be straight to shoot straight" he once said expressing his support for gays in the military.

I also got to see Senator Church that week as he ate a sandwich at his desk. In 1976, Church sought the Democratic nomination for President. He lost and also lost his Senate seat in the Reagan landslide of 1980.

Sadly, I never did get to write my book about the campaign. A journalist by the name of T.H. White scooped me with a volume, *The Making of the President 1960*; it was an instant classic. He would write several more *Making of the President* books, none however as strong as the first one.

Journal Entry for September 14
(Seeing Kennedy and Nixon)

In 1960, almost half of the states in the country were what we today would call swing states, fiercely contested. New Jersey was one of them and in fact Kennedy carried it by a margin of less than one percent. It was why I got to see Richard Nixon give a brief speech in my hometown, a speech worth recalling in the context of this campaign.

Nixon visited Plainfield, New Jersey, toward evening on October 4. He was about an hour late for the rally, apologized to the dignitaries and waiting crowd and then gave, given the lateness of the hour, what was probably an abbreviated version of his standard speech. I can still see Nixon leaning on the podium but did not hear him.

Why? This was because I was inside the barber-shop that ran along Park Avenue between Front and Second Streets getting a haircut. Today, of course, the shop would be closed and probably the subject of intense Secret Service inspection, but by then, there hadn't been a successful assassination in sixty years so a young teenager could unexpectedly look up and find himself not more than twenty-five yards from a presidential candidate, though separated by a plate glass window. I remember that the lectern had been placed on Second Street looking down toward Front Street so I had a clear view of him. A large crowd filled the space between Second and Front Streets.

Thanks to the Internet, I am today able to read the transcript of the speech I missed fifty-six years ago. Remarkably from the standpoint of today's politics, Nixon had not a word to say about John Kennedy. The speech bears about as much relation to modern politics as Old English does to the modern version. The speech in fact reads like a well-organized essay setting out the three reasons why voters should prefer him over his opponent. It could have been delivered to a high school English class, a model of logic and concision.

I also got to see John Kennedy that year, this time in New York, a state that went for Kennedy by less than six points. My father was a free-lance illustrator on retainer with a number of major publishing houses. One of them, I believe Harcourt Brace, had given him two tickets to attend a Kennedy rally at the Waldorf Astoria. Toward the end of Kennedy's speech, I eyed a stairwell that appeared to be the only way Kennedy could exit. I told my father I was going to see if I could get a closer look at the candidate by going to the stairwell. I went and I did. Indeed, if recollection serves, I was even able to hear Kennedy saying something to Jackie about meeting her later back at the hotel. In any event, I was close enough to remember the intense blue of his eyes that really did seem to sparkle and the chestnut color of his hair.

Journal Entry for September 28
(the first Presidential Debate)

In 1960, I watched the very first modern presidential debate between John Kennedy and Richard Nixon along with my parents and about a hundred others, in the small auditorium of our local Jewish Community Center on West Eighth Street in Plainfield, New Jersey. A 21-inch Black and white television had been set up on the stage; there was discussion afterwards. It was a community event. I have a warm feeling about it, even now. Nixon people actually sat next to Kennedy people. Some of them even went to each other's homes afterwards to continue the night's discussion. Friendships were not imperiled by political differences. It was also a time when, in describing someone to a friend, you didn't feel the need to immediately identify whether he or she was Republican or Democrat, nor did parents fear, as it has been well documented they do today, that their child might fall in love with someone of the opposite political persuasion. In 1960, party affiliation was regarded as just another fact about someone, not a clue to their character.

Part of the reason for that tolerance was the degree to which there was a broad consensus within the country about many things. Some of that consensus, of course, is today rightfully a source of shame or embarrassment: Blacks were still second-class citizens; gays had to hide their identities if they wanted to lead normal lives; and women were still supposed to channel all their hopes and creativity into their roles as wives and mothers. But there was a generally shared prosperity, a bi-partisan foreign policy agreed upon as absolutely necessary in light of the communist threat, and President Eisenhower had basically accepted the New Deal's administrative state. The planet's temperature also seemed about right, Vietnam was still a distant country few had heard of, and pro-choice and pro-life not yet rallying cries.

The first Kennedy/Nixon debate began with each candidate giving eight-minute opening statements. Today, in a world where many supposedly feel compelled to consult their mobile phones every five minutes, that amount of time seems unthinkable.

One reads the transcript of the first debate and is astonished by the number of times that Vice-President Nixon insists that he shares the same goals as Senator Kennedy but just disagrees as to means.

It seems incredible that a moment I remember so clearly – or more accurately I think I remember so clearly — happened more than half a century ago but that, I'm told, is what I can expect, recent events disappearing quickly from the rear view mirror, older memories looming larger and larger. Given the current [2016] campaign so far, it is not a bad trade-off.